LET THERE BE GOD

*An anthology of
modern religious poetry*

compiled by

T. H. PARKER
and
F. J. TESKEY

THE RELIGIOUS EDUCATION PRESS LTD.
(A member of the Pergamon Group)
HEADINGTON HILL HALL   OXFORD

Made and printed in Great Britain by
Cox & Wyman Limited, London, Fakenham and Reading

08 006269 5 soft cover
08 006272 5 hard cover

022467
821.08/8136

CONTENTS

CONTENTS

CONTENTS

THE MYSTIC CIRCLE

THE MYSTIC CIRCLE

'Let there be life, said God . . .
Let there be God, say I . . .
Let life be God . . .'

The Power and the Glory
Siegfrid Sassoon

Into those three short sentences Siegfrid Sassoon has com-
pressed a profound religious belief. And with many of his fellow
artists, whether they be painters, sculptors, composers, or poets,
he could have postulated, 'Let life be art', thus completing the
mystic circle: God, Life, Art.

Religion and the arts have always been naturally complementary. Temples to Athene, Parthenos and Zeus architecturally
showed the Greeks' reverence and fear for their gods; statues of
the Roman deities, Jupiter, Venus and Apollo were the fore-
runners of Epstein's *Madonna and Child* and *St. Michael and the
Devil*. A religion of love and hope was enshrined in the sublime
poetry of the Psalms, and in all ages great music has ennobled
man's idea of God. Enamel and gold of Russian icons depicted
Christ in human likeness; mosaics and marbles of Byzantine
churches and stained-glass windows of mediæval cathedrals
spelled out the Bible story in rich colours for those who were un-
able to read. The beauty of Christ's birth and his agony on the
Cross have been portrayed by every Christian nation in painting,
sculpture, or engraving.

In the widest, and possibly truest, sense of the word, all great
artists have been religious in that they have created works which
appeal, as religion does, to the best in man. It must be recognized
that man has a 'best', and by corollary, a 'worst'. That is a basic
premise whether one's ideals are Christian, Buddhist, Moslem,
Humanist, or even Existentialist.

Perhaps it is that restless 'best' in man that prompts progress.
Progress of any kind implies the existence of a desirable goal, and

I

a recognition of the defects in an existing system, whether it be an economic, a social, or a religious system.

The materialistic twentieth century sees a solution to its problems in the raising of living standards. America is lauded for its prosperity; the emergent nations of Africa clamour for a greater portion of the world's goods; Communist Russia and China are equally set on an increasing affluence.

It would be wrong to attempt to deny the validity of such attitudes; every man has a natural right to the good things of this earth. And there is sufficient for everyone, even though many sources may as yet be untapped. It is, however, still pertinent to say, 'What shall it profit a man if he gain the whole world and lose his own soul?' Materialism *per se* is barren and arid. A nation obsessed with materialism must inevitably and ultimately die. Having achieved all its material needs, it has nothing left to live for; the real goal, the ultimate vision, has disappeared. And what else is there for any generation, any country, to hand on to its children except vision, a reason for living, for striving, even for suffering? 'Where there is no vision the people perish'.

Creative artists have always realized that, either through reasoning or intuitively. But they can also see the misery and suffering, physical and spiritual, that have always been with us. Indeed, because of his sensitivity, the creative artist may be the one who suffers most. Thus arises a dichotomy: on the one hand is the visionary who can see heaven despite this world, or perhaps because of this world; on the other hand is the ordinary citizen of this world, who feels strongly the injustices of life but cannot find hope in the tangle of his frustrations because he has no vision.

One can detect those two attitudes in the poetry, the painting and the sculpture of our times. A work of art is essentially part of God, even though the tone may be bitter, cynical or ironic. The two attitudes are not mutually exclusive; they are, indeed, complementary. Man is of God, although he is but 'flesh and bone', 'Adam unparadised'. He recognizes his own sin in that he crucified God the Son; today men are still

> *onloookers at the crime*
> *Callous contemporaries of the slow torture of God.*

Every generation must find its own values; the present generation is still searching. Man, while recognizing the existence of God, queries his effectiveness, derides his divinity, sneers at his tenets. But even this is not new; nor is it vital. The fact that man may deny Christianity does not refute the existence of God, who, as D. H. Lawrence said, may exist in 'a living unconscious life. If only we were to shut our eyes; if only we were all struck blind, and things vanished from our sight, we should marvel that we have fought and lived for shallow, visual, peripheral nothingness. We should find reality in darkness'.

It is in the darkness of man's mind that God exists. His spirit is revealed through the agony of creation, whether it be of life, of poetry, of painting, of sculpture, or of music.

The poems and illustrations in *Let there be God* are selected to emphasize the impact that God has made on the twentieth-century creative artist. The mystic circle of God, Life and Art, admits of no systematic philosophy or dogmatic religious creed. God has as many faces as there are poets and painters; 'religion' is a personal feeling, and God reveals Himself in myriads of ways. Thus the poems range from the naïve but profoundly moving simplicity of *The Creation* to the sophistication of *The Transfiguration*; from the expressed doubt of *Oh Christianity, Christianity* to the calm resolution of *The Rock*; from the ironic scepticism of *Good Friday* to the unquestioning acceptance of *The Resurrection*; from the mysticism of *The Apocalypse* to the horrifying realism of *Ecce Homo*.

An equally wide variety of approach and interpretation is apparent in the illustrations. The contemporary artist, whether he is working in oils, tapestry, stone, or glass makes his own significant comment on the validity of Biblical truths. Unquestioning acceptance is rare; doubt, disillusionment, and despair are often evident. But the doubt, disillusionment, and despair spring, not from religion, but from man's approach to it and from his treatment of the living God. The artist, in whatever medium he works, depicts what he feels to be right. Society may reject his interpretation, although it cannot ignore it; here it is comment enough to say that society rejected God the Son nearly 2,000 years ago. And yet he still lives, and is honoured and glorified today in art as much as he ever was in the past. God in Art represents the best in life.

WHAT SHALL IT PROFIT A MAN . . .

OH CHRISTIANITY, CHRISTIANITY

Oh Christianity, Christianity,
Why do you not answer our difficulties?
If He was God He was not like us
He could not lose.

Can Perfection be less than perfection?
Can the creator of the Devil be bested by him?
What can the temptation to possess the earth have meant to Him
Who made and possessed it? What do you mean?

And Sin, how could He take our sins upon Him? What does it
    mean?
To take sin upon one is not the same
As to have sin inside one and feel guilty.

It is horrible to feel guilty,
We feel guilty because we are.
Was He horrible? Did He feel guilty?

You say He was born humble – but He was not,
He was born God —
Taking our nature upon Him. But then you say,
He was perfect Man. Do you mean
Perfectly Man, meaning wholly? Or Man without sin? Ah
Perfect Man without sin is not what we are.

Do you mean He did not know that He was God,
Did not know He was the Second Person of the Trinity!
(Oh and if He knew this was
It a source of strength for Him we do not have)
But this theology of emptying you preach sometimes —
That He emptied Himself of knowing that He was God – seems
A theology of false appearances
To mock your facts, as He was God whether He knew He was or
    not.

Oh what do you mean?
Oh what do you mean?

6

You never answer our difficulties.
You say, Christianity, you say
That the Trinity is unchanging from eternity,
But then you say
At the incarnation He took
Our Manhood into the Godhead
That did not have it before,
So it must have changed it,
Having it.

Oh what do you mean, what do you mean?
You never answer our questions.

Stevie Smith

THE MAMMON OF UNRIGHTEOUSNESS

I, grown old in your service, come to the temple
Seeking comfort and ease.
Not on my knees,
But proudly upright I stand
And hold out my hand
To receive the assurance of help
That has never yet failed.

All that you gave me I used, to your honour and mine.
Base metal to silver was turned, and silver to gold;
And here now, behold!
I pour it all out on your altar
And grudge not the gift.

I have walked in your laws all my days,
And followed your ways
As you bade me, and now I am old.
Turn not your face from me;
Hear the last prayer I shall make,
For your righteousness' sake.

Other gods there are here;
None but you I held dear,
And Mammon alone I have worshipped since worship began.
I whored not after Allah or Christ,
I was not enticed
By their promise of life after death,
For I knew that my god
Would give me my reward in this lite,
And I proved his word true.

I have been known as a man
Honest in thought and in deed,
Impartial with rich and with poor,
Faithful in all to your creed.

I have not regarded the plea
Of the weakling, the timid, the meek
Turning the other cheek.
I despised all such waverers, strong in the strength of my right.
I have encouraged no beggar or masterless man;
I know it is part of your plan
That all men should work for their bread.
I have been deaf to the cry
Of the widow mourning her dead
And the fatherless child,
Leaving them both to the mercy of Mammon, giver of gifts.

Have I not even
Sacrificed to you my child,
My first-born the wild,
Untameable spirit that would not bow down in your house?
Where is he now? Where are my parents, my wife,
The friends of young days —
All dead, all dispersed,
Gone unregarded while I was about your concerns,
Withered away like the flowers
I spurned, like the useless and profitless flowers —
Have I not merited praise,
Having thus set them aside that you might be first
In my thoughts, in my working, laborious hours?

Who are these men who crowd to the temple today,
With their drab ragged coats and their lustreless eyes,
Hemming me in
With their faces so ravaged and gray?

Who are these women, tight-lipped, talon-clawed,
Whose beauty has faded away?
Why are their movements uncertain,
Their voices so thin?
What canker, what sin,
Drives them to enter the precinct, and when they would pray
Clogs their reluctant tongues as they falter and fail
And cannot find words to begin?

9

LET THERE BE GOD

And am I even as they?

They drift to your feet like dead leaves,
They are brittle and sere.
Once all who worshipped you here
Were my equals in beauty and strength,
Shining in thick silken coats, with the flash of deep fire
From their jewels, the gleam of bright gold from the wall,
While the silver lamps shone on us all.
We were confident then. We knew that our god was almighty,
Omnipotent, changeless, and all that we did
Was to glorify him and was good in his sight.
But now comes the night.
The lamps are extinguished,
The golden walls tarnished,
From your image no sign, and in terror we grope—
Give us light, give us hope!
In the darkness a cry of despair,
Our words are as empty as air,
Mammon, are you there?
Where?

Now while I pour on your altar my offering of gold
Why am I lonely—and cold?

Phyllis Hartnoll

THE SON OF MAN

From His eternal seat Christ comes down to this earth, where, ages ago, in the bitter cup of death He poured his deathless life for those who came to the call and those who remained away.

He looks about Him, and sees the weapons of evil that wounded His own age.

The arrogant spikes and spears, the slim, sly knives, the scimitar in diplomatic sheath, crooked and cruel, are hissing and raining sparks as they are sharpened on monster wheels.

But the most fearful of them all, at the hands of the slaughterers, are those on which has been engraved His own name, that are fashioned from the texts of His own words fused in the fire of hatred and hammered by hypocritical greed.

He presses His hand upon His heart; He feels that the age-long moment of His death has not yet ended, that new nails, turned out in countless numbers by those who are learned in cunning craftsmanship, pierce Him in every joint.

They had hurt Him once, standing in the shadow of their temple; they are born anew in crowds.

From before their sacred altar they shout to the soldiers, 'Strike!'

And the Son of Man in agony cries, 'My God, my God, why hast Thou forsaken Me?'

Rabindranath Tagore

CHURCH GOING

Once I am sure there's nothing going on
I step inside, letting the door thud shut.
Another church: matting, seats, and stone,
And little books; sprawlings of flowers, cut
For Sunday, brownish now; some brass and stuff
Up at the holy end; the small neat organ;
And a tense, musty, unignorable silence,
Brewed God knows how long. Hatless, I take off
My cycle-clips in awkward reverence.

Move forward, run my hand around the font.
From where I stand, the roof looks almost new—
Cleaned, or restored? Someone would know: I don't.
Mounting the lectern, I peruse a few
Hectoring large-scale verses, and pronounce
'Here endeth' much louder than I'd meant.
The echoes snigger briefly. Back at the door
I sign the book, donate an Irish sixpence,
Reflect the place was not worth stopping for.

Yet stop I did: in fact I often do,
And always end much at a loss like this,
Wondering what to look for, wondering, too,
When churches fall completely out of use
What shall we turn them into, if we shall keep
A few cathedrals chronically on show,
Their parchment, plate and pyx in locked cases,
And let the rest rent-free to rain and sheep.
Shall we avoid them as unlucky places?

Or, after dark, will dubious women come
To make their children touch a particular stone;
Pick simples for a cancer; or on some
Advised night see walking a dead one?
Power of some sort or other will go on
In games, in riddles, seemingly at random;

But superstition, like belief, must die,
And what remains when disbelief has gone?
Grass, weedy pavement, bramble, buttress, sky,

A shape less recognizable each week,
A purpose more obscure. I wonder who
Will be the last, the very last, to seek
This place for what it was; one of the crew
That tap and jot and know what roof-lofts were?
Some ruin-bibber, randy for antique,
Or Christmas-addict, counting on a whiff
Of gown-and-bands and organ-pipes and myrrh?
Or will he be my representative,

Bored, uninformed, knowing the ghostly silt
Dispersed, yet tending to this cross of ground
Through suburb scrub because it held unspilt
So long and equably what since is found
Only in separation – marriage, and birth,
And death, and thoughts of these – for which was built
This special shell? For, though I've no idea
What this accoutred frowsty barn is worth,
It pleases me to stand in silence here;

A serious house on serious earth it is,
In whose blent air all our compulsions meet,
Are recognised, and robed as destinies.
And that much never can be obsolete,
Since someone will forever be surprising
A hunger in himself to be more serious,
And gravitating with it to this ground,
Which, he once heard, was proper to grow wise in,
If only that so many dead lie round.

Philip Larkin

IN THE BEGINNING...

The Cosmos
FRANK J. MALINA

THE CREATION

And God stepped out on space,
And he looked around and said:
I'm lonely—
I'll make me a world.

And as far as the eye of God could see
Darkness covered everything,
Blacker than a hundred midnights
Down in a cypress swamp.

Then God smiled,
And the light broke,
And the darkness rolled up on the one side,
And the light stood shining on the other,
And God said: That's good!

Then God reached out and took the light in his hands,
And God rolled the light around in his hands
Until he made the sun:
And he set the sun a-blazing in the heavens.
And the light that was left from making the sun
God gathered it up in a shining ball
And flung it against the darkness,
Spangling the night with the moon and stars.
Then down between
The darkness and the light
He hurled the world;
And God said: That's good!

Then God himself stepped down—
And the sun was on his right hand,
And the moon was on his left;
And the stars were clustered about his head,
And the earth was under his feet.
And God walked, and where he trod
His footsteps hollowed the valleys out
And bulged the mountains up.

Then he stopped and looked and saw
That the earth was hot and barren.
So God stepped over to the edge of the world
And he spat out the seven seas—
He batted his eyes, and the lightnings flashed—
He clapped his hands, and the thunders rolled—
And the waters above the earth came down,
The cooling waters came down.

Then the green grass sprouted,
And the little red flowers blossomed,
And the pine tree pointed his finger to the sky,
And the oak spread out his arms,
And the lakes cuddled down in the hollows of the ground,
And the rivers ran down to the sea;
And God smiled again,
And the rainbow appeared,
And curled itself around his shoulder.

Then God raised his arm and waved his hand
Over the sea and over the land,
And he said: Bring forth! Bring forth!
And quicker than God could drop his hand,
Fishes and fowls
And beasts and birds
Swam from the rivers and the seas,
Roamed the forests and the woods,
And split the air with their wings.
And God said: That's good!

Then God walked around,
And God looked around
On all that he had made.
He looked at his sun,
And he looked at his moon,
And he looked at his little stars;
And he looked on his world
With all its living things,
And God said: I'm lonely still.

Then God sat down—
On the side of a hill where he could think,
By a deep wide river he sat down;
With his head in his hands,
God thought and thought,
Till he thought: I'll make me a man!

Up from the bed of the river
God scooped the clay;
And by the bank of the river
He kneeled him down;
And there the great God Almighty
Who lit the sun and fixed it in the sky,
Who flung the stars to the most far corner of the night,
Who rounded the earth in the middle of his hand;
This Great God,
Like a mammy bending over her baby,
Kneeled down in the dust
Toiling over a lump of clay
Till he shaped it in his own image;

Then into it he blew the breath of life,
And man became a living soul.
Amen. Amen.

James Weldon Johnson

THE SEVENTH DAY

The sky is all in movement
as the warm breath of summer
chases fat flocks along the fondant
ice-silvered trails' dissolving paths.
At the sky's edge the branches toss and fall,
outlined against jay's-feather blue.
Close to me, in the grass, unceasing too,
swift ants revolve, while birds weave overhead,
across and across Penelope's loom
like deft-spun thread.

Beyond my world, remote and hidden,
uncounted constellations spin.
Under my hand, unfelt, the trodden
hot atoms dance their apoplectic reels,
taking their pattern from the stars
as, on my watch, the little black hands turn
obscurely following the wheeling sun
in the round sky's treadmill.
And in this universe of movement
I alone lie still.

Is this the centre, after all,
of all the worlds,
poised between infinitely great and small,
midway from galaxies to molecules,
the point of balance where there can be peace?
Is this seventh day the privilege
linked with the barbed goad, the divine image?
As I lie, sunwarmed, on the hill crest,
out of all God's creation in my view
only He and I can rest.

Susan Glyn

from A HYMN FOR EVE

Here in His garden water flows
bright as a stream of birds, the brown
and jewel-glitter of birds' eyes,
the grain of eyes; and here the sun,
bee-gold and swarming, murmurs on
a grass as ripe as flesh. The soil
is coarse and fragrant, and the rocks
are heavy flowers. Here how cool
and soft the fruits; how warm the cheeks
– a seraph walking shadowless—
the gentle air will press to mine.

And He who made my nakedness
a song of living warmth, my skin
fragile as windflower silver, made
my strength of body suave and white,
for Adam's and His own delight.
                I may bind
the garden round me for my dress:
the river's freshly sliding coat
spangles my body; or the wind
faint as the breathing of this hand
not on my breast but near and warm,
weaves tissues such as angels own.
Pelted with gold, by day I wear
on breast and eye and every limb
the smooth stiff texture of the sun.
This world that I am in is good.

Terence Tiller

THE ANIMALS

They do not live in the world,
Are not in time and space.
From birth to death hurled
No word do they have, not one
To plant a foot upon,
Were never in any place.

For with names the world was called
Out of the empty air,
With names was built and walled,
Line and circle and square,
Dust and emerald;
Snatched from deceiving death
By the articulate breath.

But these have never trod
Twice the familiar track,
Never never turned back
Into the memoried day.
All is new and near
In the unchanging Here
On the fifth great day of God,
That shall remain the same,
Never shall pass away.

On the sixth day we came.

Edwin Muir

THE POWER AND THE GLORY

Let there be life, said God. And what He wrought
Went past in myriad marching lives, and brought
This hour, this quiet room, and my small thought
Holding invisible vastness in its hands.

Let there be God, say I. And what I've done
Goes onward like the splendour of the sun
And rises up in rapture and is one
With the white power of conscience that commands.

Let life be God. . . . What wail of fiend or wraith
Dare mock my glorious angel where he stands
To fill my dark with fire, my heart with faith?

Siegfried Sassoon

THE APPLE TREE

Let there be Light!
In pink and white
The apple tree blooms for our delight.
In pink and white,
Its shouts unheard,
The Logos itself, the Creative Word,
Bursts from nothing; and all is stirred.
It blooms and blows and shrivels to fall
Down on the earth in a pink-white pall.
Withered? But look at each green little ball,
Crowned like a globe in the hand of God,
Each little globe in a shortening rod;

Soon to be rosy and well bestowed,
A cosmos now where the blossoms glowed
Constellated around the tree,
A cone that lifts to infinity.
Each rosy globe is as red as Mars;
And all the tree is a branch of stars.
What can we say but, 'Glory be!'
When God breaks out in an apple tree?

Oliver St. John Gogarty

IMAGINATION

The primrose shape was printed on His mind
Before the primal dawn, before the springs
And rivers gathered from imagined rain—
Before the earth was made, He knew all things.

There is no darkness in the eyes of Light,
No creature without form; before the seed,
Forests of sound and colour filled His sight—
Imagination generates the deed.

Darkly in a glass the shadows move
And in the dark we see our human race
Reflected from the archetype of Love,
And dare to dream the hidden *face to face*.

Phoebe Hesketh

CABBAGES

If God were as ungenerous as man,
He would make cabbages, to feed the kine,
On some unbeautiful and heavy plan,
Meet for mere beasts. But in His craft divine
He fashions them, and colours them instead
With gold and misty blue amid the green,
Softly with purple, gallantly with red.
He curves their leaves and traces veins between;
Bejewels them with drops of rain and dew;
Caresses them with wind, and, crowning boon,
With lunar light transfigures them anew—
Great silver roses 'neath the autumn moon.

Teresa Hooley

THE SABBATH

Waking on the Seventh Day of Creation,
  They cautiously sniffed the air:
The most fastidious nostril among them admitted
  That fellow was no longer there.

Herbivore, parasite, predator scouted,
  Migrants flew fast and far—
Not a trace of his presence: holes in the earth,
  Beaches covered with tar,

Ruins and metallic rubbish in plenty
  Were all that was left of him
Whose birth on the Sixth had made of that day
  An unnecessary interim.

Well, that fellow had never really smelled
  Like a creature who would survive:
No grace, address or faculty like those
  Born on the First Five.

Back, then, at last on a natural economy,
  Now His Impudence was gone,
Looking exactly like what it was,
  The Seventh Day went on,

Beautiful, happy, perfectly pointless . . .
  A rifle's ringing crack
Split their Arcadia wide open, cut
  Their Sabbath nonsense short.
For whom did they think they had been created?
  That fellow was back,
More bloody-minded than they remembered,
  More god-like than they thought.

                                    W. H. Auden

OF MAN'S FIRST DISOBEDIENCE . . .

Eve
ILSA RODMELL

IN THE COOL OF EVENING

I thought I heard Him calling! Did you hear
A sound? a little sound!
My curious ear
Is dinned with flying noises; and the tree
Goes – whisper, whisper, whisper, silently,
Till all its whispers spread into the sound
Of a dull roar. . . .

Lie close to the ground:
The shade is deep, and He may pass us by,
We are so very small, and His great eye,
Customed to starry majesties, may gaze
Too wide to spy us hiding in the maze:

– Ah, misery! The sun has not yet gone,
And we are naked! He may look upon
Our crouching shame! May make us stand upright,
Burning in terror – O that it were night—
He may not come. . . . What? Listen! Listen, now —
He's here! Lie closer. . . . *Adam, where art thou?*

James Stephens

IN EDEN

Before the Fall, in Eden
The apples blazed on high;
The lyric stars ran singing
Across the little sky;
And Eve's was mixt with Adam's breath
Where both lay tranquilly.

After the Fall, in Eden
Lay apples, bruised and strewn;
The stars ran off in terror;
The little sky stood lone:
And Eve and Adam woke to find
They were but flesh and bone.

A. V. Bowen

OUTSIDE EDEN

Adam

How glad I am to think that our idle life is finished for ever. I
forbid you to loiter round the Gate. There is work for you, my
woman.

I always wanted to be an honest respectable man.

And I hated dawdling about under the trees all day

Nibbling bananas and sucking grapes. Look at that cave in the
hill.

That is our future home, and you must learn to cook.

The world is a different place. The sooner you know it the better.

Eve

Eden! Eden! How the sun

Is glittering on the garden still.

Adam! Adam! You are changed.

Oh the black cave, the sullen hill.

Adam

The cave is for you, for me the hill. Be sure you remember that.

Here in the World the beasts of the World devour and are de-
voured.

Here you will have no more silly lions, tame leopards and hornless
bulls.

This is my club, this tree; and you must hide in that cave.

I shall go hunt for your meat: you will find it much wiser food

Than apples.

Eve

O my lord, you are changed.

I wish I had not learned to sin.

Morning and night I'll pray and pray:

Perhaps at last He'll let us in.

Adam

Shame! Shame! You are thinking once more of your peacocks
and swans and goldfish.

You're only an idle woman; no wife for an honest man.

If ever you try to return I'll pray to God that He kill you.

Is not our cave a good enough home? I have longed for it all my
life.

Here we can plan the world: a useful world for our sons.

Eve
And was not Eden useful too?
Did God not plan it for his men?
How short our time was in that land.
We are not happy now as then.
   Adam
Well. Well. Just settle down. I'll be as kind as I can.
You're only a woman after all. You need my protection.
Don't cry.
Everyone sooner or later must learn to know the World.
Eden was only a holiday. Now there is life, great life.
You try to kindle a fire, while I must go down to the river.
Work is the future law; Work to keep one alive;
Work to forget one's life with . . .
   Eve
         Work is the only law!
         Dreadful law and sad.
         To work, to work will be good:
         To idle will be bad.
         So our children will learn
         The ways of evil and good.
         The Evil shall have no meat:
         The Righteous shall have their food.

Harold Monro

THE ADAM UNPARADISED

Faltering, with bowed heads, our altered parents
Slowly descended from their holy hill,
All their good fortune left behind and done with,
   Out through the one-way pass

Into the dangerous world, these strange countries.
No rumour in Eden had reached the human pair
Of things not men, yet half like men, that wandered
   The earth beyond its walls;

But now they heard the mountains stirred and shaken,
All the heap'd crags re-echoing, the deep tarns
And caverns shuddering and the abysmal gorges
   With dismal drums of Dwarfs;

Or, some prodigious night, waked by a thumping
Shock as of piles being driven two miles away,
Ran till the sunrise shone upon the bouncing
   Monopods at their heels;

Or held their breath, hiding, and saw their elders,
The race of giants – the bulldozer's pace,
Heads like balloons, toad-thick, ungainly torsos —
   Dotting the plains like ricks.

They had more to fear once Cain had killed a quarter
Of human kind and stolen away, and the womb
Of an unsmiling Hominid to the turncoat
   Had littered ominous sons.

A happy noise of liquid shapes, a lapping
Of small waves up and down the hills till all
Was smooth and silver, the clear Flood ascended
   Ending that crew; but still

Memory, not built upon a fake from Piltdown,
Reaches us. We know more than bones can teach.
Eve's body's language, Seth within her quickening,
   Taught him the sickening fear.

He passed the word. Before we're born we have heard it.
Long-silenced ogres boom, voices like gongs
Reverberate in the mind, a Dwarf-drum rolls,
   Trolls wind unchancy horns.

C. S. Lewis

EVE

Eve, with her basket, was
Deep in the bells and grass,
Wading in bells and grass
Up to her knees,
Picking a dish of sweet
Berries and plums to eat,
Down in the bells and grass
Under the trees.

Mute as a mouse in a
Corner the cobra lay,
Curled round a bough of the
Cinnamon tall . . . .
Now to get even and
Humble proud Heaven and
Now was the moment or
Never at all.

'Eva!' Each syllable
Light as a flower fell,
'Eva!' he whispered the
Wondering maid,
Soft as a bubble sung
Out of a linnet's lung,
Soft and most silvery
'Eva!' he said.

Picture that orchard sprite,
Eve, with her body white,
Supple and smooth to her
Slim finger-tips,
Wondering, listening,
Listening, wondering,
Eve with a berry
Half-way to her lips.

Oh had our simple Eve
Seen through the make-believe!
Had she but known the
Pretender he was!
Out of the boughs he came,
Whispering still her name,
Tumbling in twenty rings
Into the grass.

Here was the strangest pair
In the world anywhere,
Eve in the bells and grass
Kneeling, and he
Telling his story low . . . .
Singing birds saw them go
Down the dark path to
The Blasphemous Tree.

Oh what a clatter when
Titmouse and Jenny Wren
Saw him successful and
Taking his leave!
How the birds rated him,
How they all hated him!
How they all pitied
Poor motherless Eve!

Picture her crying
Outside in the lane,
Eve, with no dish of sweet
Berries and plums to eat,
Haunting the gate of the
Orchard in vain. . . .
Picture the lewd delight
Under the hill tonight—
"Eva!" the toast goes round,
"Eva!" again.

Ralph Hodgson

ON RIGHTEOUS INDIGNATION

When Adam went from Paradise
  He saw the sword and ran;
The dreadful shape, the new device,
The pointed end of Paradise,
And saw what Peril is and Price,
  And knew he was a man.

When Adam went from Paradise,
  He turned him back and cried
For a little flower from Paradise;
There came no flower from Paradise;
The woods were dark in Paradise,
  And not a bird replied.

For only comfort or contempt,
  For jest or great reward,
Over the walls of Paradise,
The flaming gates of Paradise,
The dumb shut doors of Paradise,
  God flung the flaming sword.

It burns the hand that holds it
  More than the skull it scars;
It doubles like a snake and stings,
Yet he in whose hand it swings
He is the most masterful of things,
  A scorner of the stars.

G. K. Chesterton

ONLY MAN

Only man can fall from God
Only man.

No animal, no beast nor creeping thing
no cobra nor hyena nor scorpion nor hideous white ant
can slip entirely through the fingers of the hands of God
into the abyss of self-knowledge,
knowledge of self-apart-from-god.

For the knowledge of self-apart-from-god
is an abyss down which the soul can slip
writhing and twisting in all revolutions
of the unfinished plunge
of self-awareness, now apart from God, falling
fathomless, fathomless, self-consciousness wriggling
writhing deeper and deeper in all the minutiae of self-
    knowledge,
downward, exhaustive,
yet never, never coming to the bottom, for there is no
    bottom;
zigzagging down like the fizzle from a finished rocket
the fizzling falling fire that cannot go out, dropping
    wearily,
neither can it reach the depth
for the depth is bottomless,
so it wriggles its way even further down, further down
at last in sheer horror of not being able to leave off
knowing itself, knowing itself apart from God, falling.

D. H. Lawrence.

AND THE WATERS COVERED
THE FACE OF THE EARTH

Noah's Ark
ELISABETH BAILLON

from THE FLAMING TERRAPIN

The Ark is launched; cupped by the streaming breeze.
The stiff sails tug the long reluctant keel,
And Noah, spattered by the rising seas,
Stands with his great fist fastened to the wheel.
Like driven clouds, the waves went rustling by,
Feathered and fanned across their liquid sky,
And, like those waves, the clouds in silver bars
Creamed on the scattered shingle of the stars.
All night he watched black water coil and burn,
And the white wake of phosphorous astern
Lit up the sails and made the lanterns dim,
Until it seemed the whole sea burned for him;
Beside the keel he saw the grey sharks move,
And the long lines of fire their fins would groove,
Seemed each a ghost that followed in its sleep
Those long phantasmal coffins of the deep;
And in that death-light, as the long swell rolled,
The tarpon was a thunderbolt of gold.
Then in the long night-watches he would hear
The whinnying stallions of the wind career,
And to their lost companions, in their flight,
Whine like forlorn cicalas through the night.

Then far away, all in a curve of gold,
Flounced round with spray and frilled with curling foam,
Cleaving the ocean's flatness with its bold
Ridges of glory, rose a towering dome
As the great Terrapin, bulking on high,
Spread forth his huge dimensions on the sky.

But Noah drew his blunt stone anchor in
And heaved it at him; with a thund'rous din
The stony fluke impaled the brazen shell
And set it clanging like a surly bell.
Its impact woke the looped and lazy chain
And rattling swiftly out across the main,
Drawn by the anchor from its dark abode,

Into the light that glittering serpent flowed
Chafing the waves; then as a mustang colt,
Feeling the snaffle, lurches for a bolt—
With such a lurch, with such a frantic rear,
The Ark lunged forward on her mad career,
And the old Captain, with a grip of steel,
Laid his brown hands once more upon the wheel,
Bidding his joyous pilot haul him free
From the dead earth to dare the living sea.

Roy Campbell

THE HISTORY OF THE FLOOD

Bang Bang Bang
Said the nails in the Ark.

It's getting rather dark
Said the nails in the Ark.

For the rain is coming down
Said the nails in the Ark.

Dark and dark as sin
Said the nails in the Ark.

So won't you all come in
Said the nails in the Ark.

But only two by two
Said the nails in the Ark.

So they came in two by two,
The elephant, the kangaroo,
And the gnu,
And the little tiny shrew.

41

Then the birds
Flocked in like wingéd words:
Two racket-tailed motmots, two macaws,
Two nuthatches and two
Little bright robins.

And the reptiles: the gila monster, the slow-worm,
The green mamba, the cottonmouth, and the alligator —
All squirmed in;
And after a very lengthy walk,
Two giant Galapagos tortoises.

And the insects in their hierarchies:
A queen ant, a king ant, a queen wasp, a king wasp,
A queen bee, a king bee,
And all the beetles, bugs, and mosquitoes,
Cascaded in like glittering, murmurous jewels.

But the fish had their wish;
For the rain came down.
People began to drown:
The wicked, the rich—
They gasped out bubbles of pure gold,
Which exhalations
Rose to the constellations.

So after forty days and forty nights
They were on the waste of waters
In those cramped quarters.
It was very dark, damp, and lonely.
There was nothing to see, but only
The rain which continued to drop.
It did not stop.

So Noah sent forth a Raven. The raven said 'Kark!
I will not go back to the Ark.'
The raven was footloose,
He fed on bodies of the rich—
Rich with vitamins and goo.

They had become bloated,
And everywhere they floated.
The raven's heart was black,
He did not come back.
It was not a nice thing to do:
Which is why the raven is a token of wrath,
And creaks like a rusty gate
When he crosses your path; and Fate
Will grant you no luck that day:
The raven is fey:
You were meant to have a scare.
Fortunately in England
The raven is rather rare.

Then Noah sent forth a dove
She did not want to rove.
She longed for her love—
The other turtle dove—
(For her no other dove!)
She brought back a twig from an olive tree.
There is no more beautiful tree
Anywhere on the earth,
Even when it comes to birth
From six weeks under the sea.

She did not want to rove.
She wanted to take her rest.
And to build herself a nest
All in the olive grove.
She wanted to make love.
She thought that was the best.

The dove was not a rover;
So they knew the rain was over.
Noah and his wife got out
(They had become rather stout)
And Japhet, Ham, and Shem.
(The same could be said of them.)
They looked up at the sky.
The earth was becoming dry.

The animals came ashore—
There were more of them than before:
There were two dogs and a litter of puppies;
There was a tom-cat and two tib-cats
And two litters of kittens – cats
Do not obey regulations;
And, as you might expect,
A quantity of rabbits.

God put a rainbow in the sky.
They wondered what it was for.
They had never seen a rainbow before.
The rainbow was a sign;
It looked like a neon sign—
Seven colours arched in the skies:
What should it publicize?
They looked up with wondering eyes.

It advertises Mercy
Said the nails in the Ark.

Mercy Mercy Mercy
Said the nails in the Ark.

Our God is merciful
Said the nails in the Ark.

Merciful and gracious
Bang Bang Bang Bang.

John Heath-Stubbs

THE LATE PASSENGER

The sky was low, the sounding rain was falling dense and dark,
And Noah's sons were standing at the window of the Ark.

The beasts were in, but Japhet said, 'I see one creature more
Belated and unmated there came knocking at the door.'

'Well let him knock,' said Ham, 'Or let him drown or learn to
  swim.
We're over-crowded as it is; we've got no room for him.'

'And yet it knocks, how terribly it knocks,' said Shem, 'Its feet
Are hard as horn – but oh the air that comes from it is sweet.'

'Now hush,' said Ham, 'You'll waken Dad, and once he comes to
  see
What's at the door, it's sure to mean more work for you and me.'

Noah's voice came roaring from the darkness down below,
'Some animal is knocking. Take it in before we go.'

Ham shouted back, and savagely he nudged the other two,
'That's only Japhet knocking down a brad-nail in his shoe.'

Said Noah, 'Boys, I hear a noise that's like a horse's hoof.'
Said Ham, 'Why, that's the dreadful rain that drums upon the
  roof.'

Noah tumbled up on deck and out he put his head;
His face went grey, his knees were loosed, he tore his beard and
said,

'Look, look! It would not wait. It turns away. It takes its flight.
Fine work you've made of it, my sons, between you all tonight!

'Even if I could outrun it now, it would not turn again
– Not now. Our great discourtesy has earned its high disdain.

'Oh noble and unmated beast, my sons were all unkind;
In such a night what stable and what manger will you find?

'Oh golden hoofs, oh cataracts of mane, oh nostrils wide
With indignation! Oh the neck wave-arched, the lovely pride!

'Oh long shall be the furrows ploughed across the hearts of men
Before it comes to stable and to manger once again,

'And dark and crooked all the ways in which our race shall walk,
And shrivelled all their manhood like a flower with broken stalk,

'And all the world, oh Ham, may curse the hour when you were
    born;
Because of you the Ark must sail without the Unicorn'.

C. S. Lewis

BEFORE ARARAT

Over the leagues of lifeless sea
the white bird passed – repeatedly
the buffets of the savage wind assailed her flight;
while in the west, under the frown
of purple thunders southward rolled
along the marches of the night,
mantled in light and, like some old
rich-frescoed saint, gold-aureoled,
the sun went down.

The white bird passed: no sign was there
of living thing in all the dark
vast waters spread, and, overhead,
no sign in all the empty world of air:
no sign of land – no mountain-peak
pointed above the seas its naked reef.
no top of tallest tree from which her beak
might pluck one token-leaf:
nothing – save, far below her flying,
in the grey troughs of ocean lying,
the tempest-battered ark.

And Noah looked forth:
east, and west, and south, and north,
stretched fierce and wide
the sombre waters desolate,
while in the west the last dun light
of sun died;
and night
came down upon the world – menace, and fear, and
     hate—
through which not one star burned:
not one small lamp of hope through all the skies of fate.

And as the white bird, wearily
and heavily flying at her journey's end,
returned
and at the feet of Noah fell dead,
Noah, sighing, to his children said:
'Tomorrow, I will send
over the lifeless leagues of sea,
over the world deep-drowned in misery,
another dove:
for God is not perpetual wrath, but everlasting love.'

John Redwood Anderson

PHARAOH'S DAUGHTER

I went down by the lone lake-side,
Parted the lilies, parted the sedge,
Saw the boat petal-pale on the tide
Saw the weed cling to the water's edge.

Lotus with vagrant somnolent petal
Shaped like a lotus was this small boat,
Bright with patines of beaten metal,
Pale where the lilies burn and float.

Deep in the heart of it lay a small creature
White as white fire and blinding snow,
Red as the amaranth, god-like in feature,
Small and motionless; black as sloe

Were the open fearless eyes – I saw
All things displayed in their profound,
The eye of the beetle, the lion's maw,
Pearls in the ocean, gold underground.

The great executant in the sun
Who drummed the visible world to shape
Had laid a finger-tip, only one,
On the vine and blackened the sleeping grape.

That skin-flushed, scented warm
Became the citadel of a god
The dark precursor of a storm
Would break my nation, shard and sod.

I might have left him alone, I knew
How small and frail the seed that would
O'er-top the world and centuries through
Challenge the drummer where he stood.

But love for the small thing that so great
Would grow with time possessed me so
That I took the boat and its burning freight
To my bosom that knew the taking woe.

And taking it felt my heart grow great
With the knowledge and sorrow of time to come
And clear through the opening eastern gate
Heard like a storm in summer the drum.

Small was the boat on the sleeping water
Small and yet so easily found,
I heard the great drum thunder slaughter
The tread of armies shake the ground.

They would come like pillars of sand together
And fall and mingle and be lost,
Water would cover them, wind and weather
Build them a cenotaph free of cost.

They would lie as quiet as here lies sleeping
This small boat and its bale of fire
Over the water softly creeping
To light a nation's funeral pyre.

T. W. Ramsey

THE BURNING BUSH

When Moses, musing in the desert, found
The thorn bush spiking up from the hot ground,
And saw the branches, on a sudden, bear
The crackling yellow barberries of fire,

He searched his learning and imagination
For any logical, neat explanation,
And turned to go, but turned again and stayed,
And faced the fire and knew it for his God.

I too have seen the briar alight like coal,
The love that burns, the flesh that's ever whole,
And many times have turned and left it there,
Saying: 'It's prophecy – but metaphor'.

But stinging tongues like John the Baptist shout:
'That this is metaphor is no way out.
It's dogma too, or you make God a liar;
The bush is still a bush, and fire is fire'.

Norman Nicholson

from THE FIRSTBORN (Act 3, Scene 1)

Miriam. You're going away.
Aaron.   And so is all Israel.
We all have staves in our hands and our feet shod
For travelling; Moses' orders. He also gave
Other orders; they were very curious.
We have all to eat lambs' flesh, seasoned
With bitter herbs. As I see it, Miriam,
This is his characteristic way of achieving
Unity among us, before the event,
That we should all fill this waiting time by doing
The same thing, however trivial. And then
We have splashed the blood three times over the doorways.
That is quite inexplicable. It is drying in the night air,
At this moment, while I speak. What happens, I ask myself,
When it is dry? It means our freedom. He has told me so.
Tonight we're to go free. And when I look at him
I have to permit myself a wonderful hope.

                                        Christopher Fry

OUT OF EGYPT

When Israel out of Egypt came
   Safe in the sea they trod;
By day in cloud, by night in flame,
   Went on before them God.

He brought them with a stretched out hand
   Dry footed through the foam,
Past sword and famine, rock and sand,
   Lust and rebellion, home.

I never over Horeb heard
   The blast of advent blow;
No fire-faced prophet brought me word
   Which way behoved me go.

Ascended is the cloudy flame,
   The mount of thunder dumb;
The tokens that to Israel came,
   To me they have not come.

I see the country far away
   Where I shall never stand;
The heart goes where no footsteps may
   Into the promised land.

The realm I look upon and die
   Another man will own;
He shall attain the heaven that I
   Perish and have not known.

But I will go where they are hid
   That never were begot,
To my inheritance amid
   The nation that is not.

A. E. Housman

MOSES

He left us there, went up to Pisgah hill,
And saw the holiday land, the sabbath land,
The mild prophetic beasts, millennial herds,
The sacred lintel, over-arching tree,
The vineyards glittering on the southern slopes,
And in the midst the shining vein of water,
The river turning, turning towards its home.
Promised to us. The dream rose in his nostrils
With homely smell of wine and corn and cattle,
Byre, barn and stall, sweat-sanctified smell of peace.
He saw the tribes arrayed beside the river,
White robes and sabbath stillness, still light falling
On dark heads whitened by the desert wave,
The Sabbath of Sabbaths come and Canaan their home.
All this he saw in dreaming. But we who dream
Such common dreams and see so little saw
The battle for the land, the massacres,
The vineyards drenched in aboriginal blood,
The settlement, unsatisfactory order,
The petty wars and neighbouring jealousies
And local troubles. But we did not see,
We did not see, and Moses did not see,
The great disaster, exile, diaspora,
The holy bread of the land crumbled and broken
In Babylon, Caesarea, Alexandria
As on a splendid dish, or gnawed as offal.
Nor did we see, beyond, the ghetto rising,
Toledo, Cracow, Vienna, Budapesth,
Nor, had we seen, would we have known our people
In the wild disguises of fantastic time,
Packed in dense cities, wandering countless roads,
And not a road in the world to lead them home.
How could we have seen such things? How could we have seen
That plot of ground pledged by the God of Moses
Trampled by sequent tribes, seized and forgotten
As a child seizes and forgets a toy,
Strange languages, strange gods and customs borne

E

Over it and away with the light migrations,
Stirring each century ancestral dust.
All this was settled while we stood by Jordan
That first great day, could not be otherwise.
Moses saw that day only; we did not see it;
But now it stands becalmed in time for ever:
White robes and sabbath peace, the snow-white emblem.

Edwin Muir

THE NEW MOSES

A pillar of fire went before them by night
  A pillar of cloud by day
But the signpost at the crossroads said
  Hiroshima ten miles away.

When he came down the mountain
  With the tablets in his hand
He found them worshipping the golden calf
  So he stepped in behind the band.

With his staff he struck the rock
  Out the petrol started
Then they moved up the line of trucks
  And with full tanks departed.

He organized a service
  For gathering the quails and manna
So that they could be properly rationed
  And properly taxed. Hosanna!

But when they came to the riverside
  Lord! how their faces fell
The cherub with the fiery sword
  Was waiting there as well.

M. K. Joseph

I BRING YOU GOOD TIDINGS
OF GREAT JOY

THE ANNUNCIATION

Nothing will ease the pain to come
Though now she sits in ecstasy
And let it have its way with her.
The angel's shadow in the room
Is lightly lifted as if he
Had never terrified her there.

The furniture again returns
To its old simple state. She can
Take comfort from the things she knows
Though in her heart new loving burns,
Something she never gave to man
Or god before, and this god grows

Most like a man. She wonders how
To pray at all, what thanks to give
And whom to give them to. 'Alone
To all men's eyes I now must go,'
She thinks, 'And by myself must live
With a strange child that is my own.'

So from her ecstasy she moves
And turns to human things at last
(Announcing angels set aside).
It is a human child she loves
Though a god stirs beneath her breast
And great salvations grip her side.

Elizabeth Jennings

MARY OF NAZARETH

It was like music:
Hovering and floating there
With the sound of lutes and timbrels
In the night air.

It was like waves,
Beating upon the shore:
Insistent with a rhythm, a pulsing
Unfelt before.

It was like wind:
Blowing from off the seas
Of other, far other
Lands than these.

It was like wings,
Like whirring wings that fly—
The song of an army of swans
On the dark sky.

It was like God:
A presence of blinding light,
Ravishing body and soul
In the Spring night.

Clive Sansom

JOURNEY OF THE MAGI

'A cold coming we had of it,
Just the worst time of year
For a journey, and such a long journey:
The ways deep and the weather sharp,
The very dead of winter.'
And the camels galled, sore-footed, refractory,
Lying down in the melting snow.
There were times we regretted
The summer palaces on slopes, the terraces,
And the silken girls bringing sherbet.
Then the camel men cursing and grumbling
And running away, and wanting their liquor and women,
And the night-fires going out, and the lack of shelters,
And the cities hostile and the towns unfriendly
And the villages dirty and charging high prices:
A hard time we had of it.
At the end we preferred to travel all night,
Sleeping in snatches,
With the voices singing in our ears, saying
That this was all folly.

Then at dawn we came down to a temperate valley,
Wet, below the snow line, smelling of vegetation;
With a running stream and a water-mill beating the darkness,
And three trees on the low sky,
And an old white horse galloped away in the meadow.
Then we came to a tavern with vine-leaves over the lintel,
Six hands at an open door dicing for pieces of silver,
And feet kicking the empty wine-skins.
But there was no information, and so we continued
And arrived at evening, not a moment too soon
Finding the place; it was (you may say) satisfactory.

All this was a long time ago, I remember,
And I would do it again, but set down
This set down
This: were we led all that way for

Birth or Death? There was a Birth, certainly,
We had evidence and no doubt. I had seen birth and death,
But had thought they were different; this Birth was
Hard and bitter agony for us, like Death, our death.
We returned to our places, these Kingdoms,
But no longer at ease here, in the old dispensation,
With an alien people clutching their gods.
I should be glad of another death.

T. S. Eliot

INNOCENTS' DAY

And Herod said: 'sup-
posing you had been in my shoes, what would you have
Done different? – I was not thinking of myself. This
Child – whichever number might have come from the hat – could
Scarcely have begun to make trouble for twenty or
Thirty years at least, and by that time
Ten to one I'd be dead and gone. What
Matters is to keep a straight succession none can
Argue about – someone acceptable to the occupying
Power, who nevertheless will enable us to preserve our sense of
  being a nation,
Belonging and bound to one particular place.
I know my people. They are nomads, only
Squatters here as yet. They have never left the
Wilderness. Wherever in Asia Minor the grass
Seams a dune, or a well greens a wadi, or
Sheep can feed long enough for a tent to be pitched,
There they call home, praying for daily
Manna and a nightly pillar of fire. They are
Chronic exiles; their most-sung psalms look
Back to the time of looking back. They never see
Jerusalem in the here and now, but always long to
Be where they really are.

                                              If this child had
Lived, they'd have started the same blind trek, prospecting
In sand for their own footsteps. Yes,
Mothers are weeping in the streets of Judaea, but still the
Streets are there to weep in. If that child had lived,
Not a stone would have stayed on a stone, nor a brother with
    brother,
Nor would all the Babylons of all the world
Have had water enough to swill away their tears.

                                          That
I have put a stop to, at the price
Of a two-year crop of children, making
What future observers will undoubtedly judge a
Good bargain with history.

                                    Norman Nicholson

A SONG FOR SIMEON

Lord, the Roman hyacinths are blooming in bowls and
The winter sun creeps by the snow hills;
The stubborn season has made stand.
My life is light, waiting for the death wind,
Like a feather on the back of my hand.
Dust in sunlight and memory in corners
Wait for the wind that chills towards the dead land.

Grant us thy peace.
I have walked many years in this city,
Kept faith and fast, provided for the poor,
Have given and taken honour and ease.
There never went any rejected from my door.

Who shall remember my house, where shall live my children's
    children
When the time of sorrow is come?
They shall take to the goat's path, and the foxes' home,
Fleeing from the foreign faces and the foreign swords.

Before the time of cords and scourges and lamentation
Grant us thy peace.
Before the stations of the mountain of desolation,
Before the certain hour of maternal sorrow,
Now at this birth season of decease,
Let the Infant, the still unspeaking and unspoken Word,
Grant Israel's consolation
To one who has eighty years and no tomorrow.

According to thy word.
They shall praise Thee and suffer in every generation
With glory and derision,
Light upon light, mounting the saints' stair.
Not for me the martydom, the ecstasy of thought and prayer,
Not for me the ultimate vision.
Grant me thy peace.
(And a sword shall pierce thy heart,
Thine also).
I am tired with my own life and the lives of those after me,
I am dying in my own death and the deaths of those after me.
Let thy servant depart,
Having seen thy salvation.

T. S. Eliot

BETHLEHEM

Oh, ye, as shepherds or as kings,
That tread in hope this metalled way,
Think not to find again the cave
Where God Incarnate lay.

No breath of air from Shepherds' Fields,
No gleam of stars, no glimpse of sky,
No sound of village life comes here,
No ox or ass stands by.

But high above us towers the church,
And there the warring factions keep
Continual strife about the place
Where Peace was wont to sleep.

The floor by pilgrim feet is worn,
The stones by fervent lips are pressed,
That love their God, but cannot love
His image manifest.

And, grim reminder of the past,
A policeman in the grotto stands,
Lest those who worship God with words
Offend Him with their hands,

In anger raised to strike the blow
That brands us with the curse of Cain,
And wakes a sleeping Child to weep
And take up His Cross again.

Phyllis Hartnoll

THREE CHRISTMAS TREES

The tree of night has all its candles lit,
and dreams are piled about its foot: oh son,
oh sleeping son, what do you take from it?
There is no age in sleep; the boy is one
with infant and with patriarch: how guess
what shining branches lift, or rivers run,
on what far day, in this your timelessness?

Are you companion to that other boy
whose parents' dreams lay round him as he slept?
Between them in their sleep, what starry joy
of leaves arose, what holy river crept
– Jordan, the olives green round Galilee?
Or innocent blood, and tears, that Rachel wept;
an only gift upon a fatal tree?

Son, do not wake too early. All tonight
is yours to bid, a safe deceiver; day
with all its presents opened, every light
its coloured mystery lost, will not obey.
Late rising to your Paradise, take all
our other gifts; but let the apple stay
on that tree's bough, which breaking, you will fall.

Terence Tiller

THE CIRCLE OF A GIRL'S ARMS

The circle of a girl's arms
have changed the world
the round and sorrowful world
to a cradle of God.

She has laid love in His cradle.
In every cot,
Mary has laid her child.

In each
comes Christ.
In each Christ comes
to birth,
comes Christ from the Mother's breast,
as the bird from the sun
returning,
returning again to the tree he knows
and the nest,
to last year's rifled nest.

Into our hands
Mary has given her child,
heir to the world's tears,
heir to the world's toil,
heir to the world's scars,
heir to the chill dawn
over the ruin of wars.

She has laid love in His cradle,
answering for us all.
'Be it done unto me.'

The child in the wooden bed,
the light in the dark house,
the life in the fainting soul,

the Host in the priest's hands,
the seed in the hard earth,
the man who is child again,
quiet in the burial bands
waiting his birth.

Mary, Mother of God,
we are the poor soil
and the dry dust,
we are hard with a cold frost.

Be warmth to the world,
be the thaw,
warm on the cold frost,
be the thaw that melts.
That the tender shoot of Christ,
piercing the hard heart,
flower to a spring in us.

Be the hands that are rocking the world
to a kind rhythm of love;
that the incoherence of war
and the chaos of our unrest
be soothed to a lullaby,
and the round and sorrowful world
in your hands,
the cradle of God.

Caryll Houselander

EPSTEIN'S MADONNA AND CHILD

Dear Son of the world, are you still in your swaddling bands
   Or do these bands foreshadow your winding sheet?
Unpierced are yet your feet, your side, your hands—
   Oh! infinitely pathetic are your feet
Hanging beside your mother's! She endures
   Resigned and loyal in her impending loss;
'Here I present,' she says, 'my Son and yours.
   He is as yet too little for the Cross.'

In that thin form we passers-by behold
   The Man foreshadowed in the Boy confessed,
And in the living lead the gleam of gold;
   And on those lips still warm from his mother's breast
Tremble the words that would the world enfold—
   'Come unto me . . . and I will give you rest.'

Geoffrey Dearmer

A WEEK TO CHRISTMAS from Autumn Journal

A week to Christmas, cards and snow and holly,
  Gimcracks in the shops,
Wishes and memories wrapped in tissue paper,
  Trinkets, gadgets and lollipops
And as if through coloured glasses
  We remember our childhood's thrill
Waking in the morning to the rustling of paper,
  The eiderdown heaped in a hill
Of wogs and dogs and bears and brick and apples
  And the feeling that Christmas Day
Was a coral island in time where we land and eat our lotus
  But where we can never stay.
There was a star in the East, the magi in their turbans
  Brought their luxury toys
In homage to a child born to capsize their values
  And wreck their equipoise.
A smell of hay like peace in the dark stable—
  Not peace however but a sword
To cut the Gordian knot of logical self-interest,
  The fool-proof golden cord;
For Christ walked in where no philosopher treads
  But armed with more than folly,
Making the smooth place rough and knocking the heads
  Of Church and State together.
In honour of whom we have taken over the pagan
  Saturnalia for our annual treat
Letting the belly have its say, ignoring
  The spirit while we eat.
And Conscience still goes crying through the desert
  With sackcloth round his loins:
A week to Christmas – hark the herald angels
  Beg for copper coins.

Louis MacNeice

ST. JOHN BAPTIST

I, John, not reed but root;
Not vested priest nor saviour but a voice
Crying daylong like a cricket in the heat,
Demand your worship. Not of me
But of the traveller I am calling
From beyond Jordan and the limestone hills,
Whose runner and rude servant I am only.
Not man entirely but God's watchman,
I dwell among these blistered rocks
Awaiting the wide dawn, the wonder
Of His first coming, and the Dove's descent.

Sidney Keyes

JESUS AND HIS MOTHER

My only son, more God's than mine,
Stay in this garden ripe with pears.
The yielding of their substance wears
A modest and contented shine:
And when they weep with age, not brine
But lazy syrup are their tears.
'I am my own and not my own.'

He seemed much like another man,
That silent foreigner who trod
Outside my door with lily rod:
How could I know what I began
Meeting the eyes more furious than
The eyes of Joseph, those of God?
'I was my own and not my own.'

And who are these twelve labouring men?
I do not understand your words:
I taught you speech, we named the birds,
You marked their big migrations then
Like any child. So turn again
To silence from the place of crowds.
'I am my own and not my own.'

Why are you sullen when I speak?
Here are your tools, the saw and knife
And hammer on your bench. Your life
Is measured here in week and week
Planed as the furniture you make,
And I will teach you like a wife
To be my own and all my own.

Who like an arrogant wind blown
Where he may please, needs no content?
Yet I remember how you went
To speak with scholars in furred gown.
I hear an outcry in the town;
Who carried that dark instrument?
'One all his own and not his own.'

Treading the green and nimble sward,
I stare at a strange shadow thrown.
Are you the boy I bore alone,
No doctor near to cut the cord?
I cannot reach to call you Lord,
Answer me as my only son.
'I am my own and not my own.'

Thom Gunn

IN THE WILDERNESS

Christ of His gentleness
Thirsting and hungering,
Walked in the wilderness;
Soft words of grace He spoke
Unto lost desert-folk
That listened wondering.
He heard the bitterns call
From ruined palace-wall,
Answered them brotherly
He held communion
With the she-pelican
Of lonely piety.
Basilisk, cockatrice,
Flocked to His homilies,
With mail of dread device,
With monstrous barbèd stings,
With eager dragon-eyes;
Great bats on leather wings,
And poor blind broken things,
Foul in their miseries.
And ever with Him went,
Of all His wanderings
Comrade, with ragged coat,
Gaunt ribs – poor innocent —
Bleeding foot, burning throat,
The guileless old scape-goat;
For forty days and nights
Followed in Jesus' ways,
Sure guard behind him kept,
Tears like a lover wept.

Robert Graves

RETRO ME, SATHANAS

How strange of the Devil
With his unerring aptitude for putting the wrong thing in the
   right place,
To try to tempt Christ
With all the kingdoms of the world and the glory thereof.

He might have guessed
That a soul so ancient,
Treading the echoing corridors of the past to its last goal of
   simplicity, lowliness and degradation,
Would in its journey,
Have worn the purple of kings,
The scarlet of conquerors,
Would have known all pride, pomp, wealth and dominion,
Weighing them less, in its final immense cumulative wisdom,
Than the feather of a sparrow or the petal of a poppy in the corn.
He might have been sure
That it is no use bribing God with unrealities.

He should have offered Him
A quiet cottage in Nazareth,
A little child listening to the birds,
And a patch of field flowers.

Teresa Hooley

THE TRANSFIGURATION

So from the ground we felt that virtue branch
Through all our veins till we were whole, our wrists
As fresh and pure as water from a well,
Our hands made new to handle holy things,
The source of all our seeing rinsed and cleansed
Till earth and light and water entering there
Gave back to us the clear unfallen world.
We would have thrown our clothes away for lightness,
But that even they, though sour and travel stained,
Seemed, like our flesh, made of immortal substance,
And the soiled flax and wool lay light upon us
Like friendly wonders, flower and flock entwined
As in a morning field. Was it a vision?
Or did we see that day the unseeable
One glory of the everlasting world
Perpetually at work, though never seen
Since Eden locked the gate that's everywhere
And nowhere? Was the change in us alone,
And the enormous earth still left forlorn,
An exile or a prisoner? Yet the world
We saw that day made this unreal, for all
Was in its place. The painted animals
Assembled there in gentle congregations,
Or sought apart their leafy oratories,
Or walked in peace, the wild and tame together,
As if, also for them, the day had come.
The shepherds' hovels shone, for underneath
The soot we saw the stone clear at the heart
As on the starting-day. The refuse heaps
Were grained with that fine dust that made the world;
For he had said, 'To the pure all things are pure.'
And when we went into the town, he with us,
The lurkers under doorways, murderers,
With rags tied round their feet for silence, came
Out of themselves to us and were with us,
And those who hide within the labyrinth
Of their own loneliness and gentleness came,

And those entangled in their own devices,
The silent and the garrulous liars, all
Stepped out of their own dungeons and were free.
Reality or vision, this we have seen.
If it had lasted but another moment
It might have held for ever! But the world
Rolled back into its place, and we are here,
And all that radiant kingdom lies forlorn,
As if it had never stirred; no human voice
Is heard among its meadows, but it speaks
To itself alone, alone it flowers and shines
And blossoms for itself while time runs on.

But he will come again, it's said, though not
Unwanted and unsummoned; for all things,
Beasts of the field, and woods, and rocks, and seas,
And all mankind from end to end of earth
Will call him with one voice. In our own time,
Some say, or at a time when time is ripe.
Then he will come, Christ the uncrucified,
Christ the discrucified, his death undone,
His agony unmade, his cross dismantled—
Glad to be so – and the tormented wood
Will cure its hurt and grow into a tree
In a green springtime corner of your Eden,
And Judas damned take his long journey backward
From darkness into light and be a child
Beside his mother's knee, and the betrayal
Be quite undone and never more be done.

Edwin Muir

MARTHA OF BETHANY

It's all very well
Sitting in the shade of the courtyard
Talking about your souls.
Someone's got to see to the cooking,
Standing at the oven all morning
With you two taking your ease.
It's all very well
Saying he'd be content
With bread and honey.
Perhaps he would – but I wouldn't,
Coming to our house like this,
Not giving him of our best.
Yes, it's all very well
Him trying to excuse you,
Saying your recipe's best,
Saying I worry too much,
That I'm always anxious.
Someone's got to worry—
And double if the others don't care.
For it's all very well
Talking of faith and belief,
But what would you do
If everyone sat in the cool
Not getting their meals?
And he can't go wandering and preaching
On an empty stomach—
He'd die in the first fortnight.
Then where would you be
With all your discussions and questions
And no one to answer them?
It's all very well.

Clive Sansom

LAZARUS

It was the amazing white, it was the way he simply
Refused to answer our questions, it was the cold pale glance
Of death upon him, the smell of death that truly
Declared his rising to us. It was no chance
Happening, as a man may fill a silence
Between two heart-beats, seemed to be dead and then
Astonished us with the closeness of his presence;
This man was dead, I say it again and again.
All of our sweating bodies moved towards him
And our minds moved too, hungry for finished faith.
He would not enter our world at once with words
That we might be tempted to twist or argue with:
Cold like a white root pressed in the bowels of the earth
He looked, but also vulnerable – like birth.

Elizabeth Jennings

LAZARUS NOT RAISED

He was not changed. His friends around the grave
Stared down upon his greasy placid face
Bobbing on shadows; nothing it seemed could save
His body now from the sand below their wave,
The scheduled miracle not taking place.

He lay inert beneath those outstretched hands
Which beckoned him to life. Though coffin-case
Was ready to hold life and winding-bands
At his first stir would loose the frozen glands,
The scheduled miracle did not take place.

O Lazarus, distended body laid
Glittering without weight on death's surface:
Rise now before you sink, we dare not wade
Into that sand marsh where (the mourners cried)
The scheduled miracle cannot take place.

When first aroused and given thoughts and breath,
He chose to amble at his normal pace
In childhood fields imaginary and safe—
Much like the trivial territory of death
(The miracle had not yet taken place);

He chose to spend his thoughts like this at first
And disregard the nag of offered grace,
Then chose to spend the rest of them in rest.
The final effort came, forward we pressed
To see the scheduled miracle take place:

Abruptly the corpse blinked and shook his head
Then sank again, sliding without a trace
From sight, to take slime on the deepest bed
Of vacancy. He had chosen to stay dead,
The scheduled miracle did not take place.

Nothing else changed. I saw somebody peer
Stooping, into the oblong box of space.
His friends had done their best: without such fear,
Without the terrified awakening glare,
The scheduled miracle would have taken place.

Thom Gunn

BALLAD OF THE BREAD MAN

Mary stood in the kitchen
Baking a loaf of bread.
An angel flew in through the window.
We've a job for you, he said.

God in his big gold heaven,
Sitting in his big blue chair,
Wanted a mother for his little son.
Suddenly saw you there.

Mary shook and trembled,
It isn't true what you say.
Don't say that, said the angel.
The baby's on its way.

Joseph was in the workshop
Planing a piece of wood.
The old man's past it, the neighbours said.
That girl's been up to no good.

And who was that elegant feller,
They said, in the shiny gear?
The things they said about Gabriel
Were hardly fit to hear.

Mary never answered,
Mary never replied.
She kept the information,
Like the baby, safe inside.

It was election winter.
They went to vote in town.
When Mary found her time had come
The hotels let her down.

The baby was born in an annex
Next to the local pub.
At midnight a delegation
Turned up from the Farmers' Club.

They talked about an explosion
That cracked a hole in the sky,
Said they'd been sent to the Lamb & Flag
To see god come down from on high.

A few days later a bishop
And a five-star general were seen
With the head of an African country
In a bullet-proof limousine.

We've come, they said, with tokens
For the little boy to choose.
Told the tale about war and peace
In the television news.

After them came the soldiers
With rifle and bomb and gun,
Looking for enemies of the state.
The family had packed and gone.

When they got back to the village
The neighbours said to a man
That boy will never be one of us
Though he does what he blessed well can.

He went round to all the people
A paper crown on his head.
Here is some bread from my father.
Take, eat, he said.

Nobody seemed very hungry.
Nobody seemed to care.
Nobody saw the god in himself
Quietly standing there.

He finished up in the papers.
He came to a very bad end.
He was charged with bringing the living to life.
No man was that prisoner's friend.

There's only one kind of punishment
To fit that kind of a crime.
They rigged a trial and shot him dead.
They were only just in time.

They lifted the young man by the leg,
They lifted him by the arm,
They locked him in the cathedral
In case he came to harm.

They stored him as safe as water
Under seven rocks.
One Sunday morning he burst out
Like a jack-in-the-box.

Through the town he went walking.
He showed them holes in his head.
Now do you want any loaves? he cried.
Not today, they said.

Charles Causley

THE DONKEY'S OWNER

Snaffled my donkey, he did – good luck to him!—
Rode him astride, feet dangling, near scraping the ground.
Gave me the laugh of my life when I first see them,
Remembering yesterday – you know, how Pilate come
Bouncing along the same road, only that horse of his
Big as a bloody house and the armour shining
And half Rome trotting behind. Tight-mouthed he was,
Looking he owned the world.
                                    Then today,
Him and my little donkey! Ha – laugh?—
I thought I'd kill myself when he first started.
So did the rest of them. Gave him a cheer
Like he was Caesar himself, only more hearty:
Tore off some palm-twigs and followed shouting,
Whacking the donkey's behind. . . . Then suddenly
We see his face.
The smile had gone, and somehow the way he sat
Was different – like he was much older – you know—
Didn't want to laugh no more.

Clive Sansom

THE TOWER

It was deep night, and over Jerusalem's low roofs
The moon floated, drifting through the high vaporous woofs.
The moonlight crept and glistened silent, solemn, sweet,
Over dome and column, up empty, endless street;
In the closed, scented gardens the rose loosed from the stem
Her white showery petals; none regarded them;
The starry thicket breathed odours to the sentinel palm;
Silence possessed the city like a soul possessed by calm.

Not a spark in the warren under the giant night,
Save where in a turret's lantern beamed a grave, still light;
There in the topmost chamber a gold-eyed lamp was lit—
Marvellous lamp in darkness, informing, redeeming it.
For, set in that tiny chamber, Jesus, the blessed and doomed,
Spoke to the lone apostles as light to men entombed;
And spreading His hands in blessing, as one soon to be dead,
He put soft enchantment into spare wine and bread.

The hearts of the disciples were broken and full of tears,
Because their Lord, the spearless, was hedged about with spears;
And in His face the sickness of departure had spread a gloom,
At leaving his young friends friendless.
                        They could not forget the tomb.

He smiled subduedly, telling in tones soft as voice of dove,
The endlessness of sorrow, the eternal solace of love;
And lifting the earthly tokens, wine and sorrowful bread,
He bade them sup and remember One who lived and was dead.
And they could not restrain their weeping.
                             But one rose up to depart,
Having weakness and hate of weakness raging within his heart,
And bowed to the robed assembly whose eyes gleamed wet in the
    light.
Judas arose and departed: night went out to the night.

Then Jesus lifted his voice like a fountain in an ocean of tears,
And comforted His disciples and calmed and allayed their fears.
But Judas wound down the turret, creeping from floor to floor,
And would fly; but one leaning, weeping, barred him beside the
    door.
And he knew her by her ruddy garment and two yet-watching
    men:
Mary of Seven Evils, Mary Magdalen.
And he was frightened at her. She sighed: 'I dreamed him dead.
We sell the body for silver . . .'
                      Then Judas cries out and fled.
Forth into the night! . . . The moon had begun to set:
A drear, deft wind went sifting, setting the dust afret;
Into the heart of the city Judas ran on and prayed
To stern Jehovah lest his deed make him afraid.

But in the tiny lantern, hanging as if on air,
The disciples sat unspeaking. Amaze and peace were there.
For *His* voice, more lovely than song of all earthly birds,
In accents humble and happy spoke slow, consoling words.

Thus Jesus discoursed, and was silent, sitting upright, and soon
Past the casement behind Him slanted the sinking moon;
And rising from Olivet, all stared, between love and dread,
—Seeing the torrid moon a ruddy halo behind His head.

                                         Robert Nichols

JUDAS ISCARIOT

The eyes of twenty centuries
  Pursue me along the corridors to where
I am painted at their ends on many walls.
  Ever-revolving futures recognize
This red hair and red beard, where I am seated
Within the dark cave of the feast of light.
  Out of my heart-shaped shadow I stretch my hand
Across the white table into the dish
But not to dip the bread. It is as though
The cloth on each side of one dove-bright face
Spread dazzling wings on which the apostles ride
Uplifting them into the vision
Where their eyes watch themselves enthroned.
  My russet hand across the dish
Plucks enviously against one feather
– But still the rushing wings spurn me below!

                 Saint Sebastian of wickedness
I stand: all eyes legitimate arrows piercing through
The darkness of my wickedness. They recognize
My halo hammered from thirty silver pieces
And the hemp rope about my neck
Soft as that Spring's hanging arms
When on my cheek he answered with the kiss
Which cuts for ever—
                 My strange stigmata,
All love and hate, all fire and ice!

  But who betrayed whom? O you,
Whose light gaze forms the azure corridor
Through which those other pouring eyes
Arrow into me – answer! Who
Betrayed whom? Who had foreseen
All, from the first? Who read
In his mind's light from the first day
That the kingdom of heaven on earth must always
Reiterate the garden of Eden,
And each day's revolution be betrayed
Within man's heart, each day?

Who wrapped
The whispering serpent round the tree
And hung between the leaves the glittering purse
And trapped the fangs with God-appointed poison?
Who knew
I must betray the truth, and made the lie
Betray its truth in me?

Those hypocrite eyes which aimed at you
Now aim at me. And yet, beyond their world
We are alone, eternal opposites,
Each turning on his pole of truth, your pole
Invisible light, and mine
Becoming what man is. We stare
Across two thousand years, and heaven, and hell,
Into each other's gaze.

Stephen Spender

CENA

A crowded Last
Supper, thirteen heads,
Twenty-six hands, some
Under the table's
Long linenfold skirts,
Elbows getting in the way,
Feet in sandals kicked
Under the stout trestles,
Fingers dipped in dishes,
Breaking bread, carafe
Decanting acid wine,
Dark, muddy, poor stuff,
John, James, Judas,
Even the betrayer
His face tanned by a golden halo
Turned all in profile
And the thirteen auras
All at different heights
Bob and jostle above
The tablecloth's white Jordan
Like balloons, buoys, mooring lights.

In mid-channel
One full face
In solitude.

James Kirkup

from NICODEMUS

Prelude 1

In a house. Darkness; then a spot of light discloses JOHN, *as an old man, writing his Gospel; he sits at the side.*

JOHN: Now when he was in Jerusalem at the passover, in the feast day, many believed in his name, when they saw the miracles which he did. But Jesus did not commit himself unto them, because he knew all men, and needed not that any should testify of man: for he knew what was in man. There was a man of the Pharisees, named Nicodemus, a ruler of the Jews; the same came to Jesus by night and said unto him—

> What did he say?—
> Where are the notes that Peter sent from Rome?
> – He too was crucified – I see
> He writes a sprawling hand like Paul. – 'Rabbi
> We know that thou art a teacher come from God.'
> And what did Jesus say? 'Except a man
> Be born again—'; that puzzled Nicodemus.
> 'How can a man be born when he is old?'
> I was not born till I was nearly thirty;
> Poor Nicodemus had a lot to learn.
> Then Jesus spoke about the wind. 'The wind—'
> He said, 'it bloweth where it listeth—'
> That was a night of wind; I thought the wind
> Would blow the Paschal moon out of the sky;
> Trees kept their backs to it, bending like divers
> But we were snug indoors; we felt it strange,
> We fishermen, to be there in the city,
> Not in the wave-lit darkness of the lake.
> It was the night that Simon cooked the supper;
> He raised the cover from a dish of eels;
> 'See, they have lost their heads like John the Baptist.'
> Said Andrew; and we all looked grave at first,
> Till Jesus smiled, then we burst out laughing.
> Fishers of men!

We little thought of the rich lustrous fish
That even then was nosing at the net.
Supper was ended and we sang our hymn;
The hymn we often sang;
We were a happy band of brothers then;
      'Behold how good a thing it is,
        and how becoming well'—
No sooner had we sung it than a knock
Came at the door. 'Go, John,' the Master said,
'We have a visitor; see who he is.'

Andrew Young

OH DEATH WHERE IS THY STING?

from RESURRECTION An Easter Sequence

It was a lovely night,
A night for weddings and for water.
Going out into the cold glow he felt washed
And clean of people. The garden had an air
Of waiting about it, as if the leaves were bent
On eavesdropping. And the rain
Scented the air with more-than-midnight pain.
And the wet trees that had nowhere to go
Stood around and gazed at the One walking there below
In agony. Ebb and flow, to and fro, Yes and No;
Doubt assailed him. Which and what to do? This much must be
    admitted,
We live between two worlds, faith and doubt,
Like breath. The air that one breathes does not care
Whether it's in or out; it's not in love with life
Or death. And yet we do not dare to hold it long,
But must let go to find again. So with faith,
With love, with everything. Now at the cross-roads,
Middled and muddled he stood.
This was it. And it was night. 'Nevertheless Thy will be done.'
That thought made morning of it, gave him ease, and issue.
He knew now how to stay and stare it out
And already the torches approached the garden.

W. R. Rodgers

SIMON THE CYRENIAN SPEAKS

He never spoke a word to me,
   And yet he called my name;
He never gave a sign to me,
   And yet I knew and came.

At first I said 'I will not bear
   His cross upon my back;
He only seeks to place it there,
   Because my skin is black.'

But he was dying for a dream,
   And he was very meek,
And in His eyes there shone a gleam
   Men journey far to seek.

It was Himself my pity bought;
   I did for Christ alone
What all of Rome could not have wrought
   With bruise of lash or stone.

Countee Cullen

THE CENTURION

What is it now? More trouble?
Another Jew? I might have known it.
These Jews, they buzz around the tail of trouble
Like lascivious flies. Do they think we're here
Because we love them? Is it their climate
That holds us here? Why, think, Marcellus—
By God, just dream of it. Today in Rome,
Less than two thousand thirsty miles away,
Fountains and squares and shadowed colonnades,
Men with smooth chins and girls that sometimes wash.
Well, who is it? . . . I see.
Another to be taken to that bonehill.
They're coming now. Just listen to them!—
You'd think they had a dozen there at least.
My sword, Marcellus. I'll be back to dinner,
Unless this fellow's a reluctant dier
Who loves the world too well.

Halt! Stop that shouting. Why is he dressed like that?
(His robes are purple. On his head
A hedge-crown. Where the thorns are driven
Berries of blood leap up . . .) 'My orders differ.
Remove that crown – at once – return his clothes.
Kingship can wait until his throne is ready.
Till then, safe conduct. Hold your lines—
Especially that to the windward: I've no fondness
For foreign spittle. Hold them. March . . .'

'Halt! Here's the place. Set down the cross.
You three attend to it. And remember, Marcus,
The blows are struck, the nails are driven
For Roman law and Roman order,
Not for your private satisfaction.
Set to work.'
(The grass is bare, sand-coloured: the hill
Quivers with heat.) 'What? As you please.

Seamless? Then dice for it.' (The sun
Is brutal in this land, metallic.
It works for death, not life.) 'Well, is it done?
Now nail the board above: "King of the Jews."
That turns the mockery on them. Watch them wince
At the superscription. Look, their faces!
Hate. Which man is hated most,
Myself or him? He'll serve for both:
They know their limitations. They know,
Greek, Jew or Roman, there is one command,
One only. What's his name?—
He takes it quietly. From Nazareth?
I know it well. Who would exchange it
For this sad city, and become
The food of flies? Marcus, there!
Give him some wine: he won't last long.'
That strain of wrist, the arms' tension
And scarecrow hang of chest. Ah well,
Poor devil, he's got decent eyes.

Clive Sansom

FATHER TO THE MAN

I warned the parents, you know,
when he was a child. I said

This boy must really not be allowed
to argue about the law with lawyers and about God
with theologians. And he seems, I said,
to fancy himself as a doctor, too. At this rate
we shall have him, perhaps, giving water
to a feverish patient. Little thinking
he'd do just that; and was lucky
the lad recovered.

It will come to no good, I said.
But one gets no thanks.

And so it went on
until, later, we lost touch;
for he was away for some years,
no one knew where.

Afterwards, I admit, I was half convinced. More than half,
I suppose I should say.

When he preached – and I shall hear no such sermons again –
it seemed that immutable right and wrong –
no, it was not that their boundaries changed. But somehow
acts and facts seemed with a shake of a word
to fall – I saw such a toy once, of foolish beads –
in a different pattern. What was done was the same,
and right and wrong were the same, and yet
not the same, being done in a different world.

There was a wedding, for instance,
with, in plain Aramaic, too much drink,
and you know the country customs—
I fear the old Gods are by no means dead.
Well, he was there, and he preached on the sabbath,
and spoke, just in passing, about the wedding;

and, you know, these junketings (to call them no worse)
seemed transformed, seemed a part
(like David's dancing in the Temple)
of our holy religion; and,
what was stranger, our religion
seemed to have grown, and to be our life.

Well, you see, it has come to no good,
as I told his parents, children
must listen, and lawful authority speak.

. . . and yet
this is the saddest news . . . and I
am nearer to death . . .

John Knight

ECCE HOMO

Whose is this horrifying face,
This putrid flesh, discoloured, flayed,
Fed on by flies, scorched by the sun?
Whose are those hollow red-filmed eyes
And thorn-spiked head and spear-struck side?
Behold the Man: He is Man's Son.

Forget the legend, tear the decent veil
That cowardice or interest devised
To make their mortal enemy a friend,
To hide the bitter truth all His wounds tell.
Let the great scandal be no more disguised:
He is in agony till the world's end,

And we must never sleep during that time!
He is suspended on the cross-tree now
And we are onlookers at the crime,
Callous contemporaries of the slow
Torture of God. Here is the hill
Made ghastly by His spattered blood

Whereon He hangs and suffers still:
See, the centurions wear riding-boots,
Black shirts and badges and peaked caps,
Greet one another with raised-arm salutes;
They have cold eyes, unsmiling lips;
Yes these his brothers know not what they do.

And on his either side hang dead
A labourer and a factory hand,
Or one is maybe a lynched Jew
And one a Negro or a Red,
Coolie or Ethiopian, Irishman,
Spaniard or German democrat.

Behind His lolling head the sky
Glares like a fiery cataract
Red with the murders of two thousand years
Committed in His name and by
Crusaders, Christian warriors
Defending faith and property.

Amid the plain beneath His transfixed hands,
Exuding darkness as indelible
As guilty stains, fanned by funereal
And lurid airs, besieged by drifting sands
And clefted landslides our about-to-be
Bombed and abandoned cities stand.

He who wept for Jerusalem
Now sees His prophecy extend
Across the greatest cities of the world,
A guilty panic reason cannot stem
Rising to raze them all as He foretold;
And He must watch this drama to the end.

Though often named, He is unknown
To the dark kingdoms at His feet
Where everything disparages His words,
And each man bears the common guilt alone
And goes blindfolded to his fate,
And fear and greed are sovereign lords.

The turning point of history
Must come. Yet the complacent and the proud
And who exploit and kill, may be denied—
Christ of Revolution and of Poetry—
The resurrection and the life
Wrought by your spirit's blood.

Involved in their own sophistry
The black priest and the upright man
Faced by subversive truth shall be struck dumb,
Christ of Revolution and of Poetry,
While the rejected and condemned become
Agents of the divine.

Not from a monstrance silver-wrought
But from the tree of human pain
Redeem our sterile misery,
Christ of Revolution and of Poetry,
That man's long journey through the night
May not have been in vain.

David Gascoyne

THE JUDAS TREE

Listen! The hounds of the judge and the priest
Are on the scent; blow your horn, make haste
Or you'll not be in at the death of Christ.

A red fox barks in Gethsemane;
Quick, he is also brought to bay
Under the roots of the Judas tree.

Who dies tonight, a man or God?
I only know the price on his head
Will buy for us all a field of blood;

But the coins of silver stick to my hand
And fester there like the crust of a wound.
The huntsmen of God, dead-drunk and blind,

Cry 'View halloo' as away they go
Over the plains of Jericho;
Red footprints murder the naked snow.

On the door of my heart the High Priest knocks,
'I am Caiaphas, Sir, I seek the fox
That has gone to ground in your brain and sex.'

OH DEATH WHERE IS THY STING?

'I have nothing to hide!' The night extends
A tree which bleeds from its human hands;
Under its branches a curtain rends,

And the soldiers rattle, one, two, three,
On the hill-top, their dice of ivory;
'I am Judas, why do you point at me?'
(Cyanide, Monoxide, Xyclon. B)

'Who is it walks?'
                        'The night is young.
Listen, the hounds are giving tongue
And the ladder I climb has a missing rung.'

Thorn, thorn, thorn, thorn, why do you stick
In my forehead like this? Thorn, thorn, I choke.
Thorn, thorn, you hang me by the neck.

Quick, quick, a fox in Gethsemane
By the hounds of God is brought to bay
Under the roots of the Judas tree.

Thomas Blackburn

BALLAD OF THE GOODLY FERE

(Simon Zelotes Speaketh it Somewhile After the Crucifixion)

Ha' we lost the goodliest fere o' all
For the priests and the gallow tree?
Aye lover he was of brawny men,
O' ships and the open sea.

When they came wi' a host to take Our Man
His smile was good to see,
'First let these go!' quo' our Goodly Fere,
'Or I'll see ye damned,' says he.

Aye he sent us out through the crossed high spears
And the scorn of his laugh rang free,
'Why took yet not me when I walked about
Alone in the town?' says he.

Oh we drunk his 'Hale' in the good red wine
When we last made company,
No capon priest was the Goodly Fere,
But a man o' men was he.

I ha' seen him drive a hundred men
Wi' a bundle of cords swung free,
That they took the high and holy house
For their pawn and treasury.

They'll no get him a' in a book I think
Though they write it cunningly;
No mouse of the scrolls was the Goodly Fere
But aye loved the open sea.

If they think they ha' snared our Goodly Fere
They are fools to the last degree.
'I'll go to the feast,' quo' our Goodly Fere,
'Though I go to the gallows tree.'

'Ye ha' seen me heal the lame and blind,
And wake the dead,' says he.
'Ye shall see one thing to master all:
'Tis how a brave man dies on the tree.'

A son of God was the Goodly Fere
That bade us his brothers be.
I ha' seen him cow a thousand men.
I have seen him upon the tree.

He cried no cry when they drave the nails
And the blood gushed hot and free,
The hounds of the crimson sky gave tongue,
But never a cry cried he.

I ha' seen him cow a thousand men
On the hills o' Galilee,
They whined as he walked out calm between,
Wi' his eyes like the grey o' the sea.

Like the sea that brooks no voyaging
With the winds unleashed and free,
Like the sea that he cowed at Genesaret
Wi' twey words spoke' suddenly.

A master of men was the Goodly Fere,
A mate of the wind and the sea,
If they think they ha' slain our Goodly Fere
They are fools eternally.

I ha' seen him eat o' the honey-comb
Sin' they nailed him to the tree.

Ezra Pound

THE CRUCIFIXION

From the first He would not avoid it.
He knew they would stone and defile Him, and looked to it calmly,
Riding to meet it serenely across the palm leaves,—
Processions in the East being near to bloodshed,—
Foreseeing a time when the body and all its injunctions
And *life* and *people* and all their persistent demands
Would desist, and they'd leave a policeman
Outside his door or his tomb to keep all in order
While he lay in supremest consummate passion
Passively passionate, suffering suffering only.

And this surrender of self to a greater statement
Has been desired by many more humble than he.
But when it came, was it other than he had imagined?
Breaking his Self up, convulsing his Father in pain?
His will prevented by every throbbing stigma,
The pangs that puffed and strained his stomach wall,
The utter weariness that bowed his head,
Taught him perhaps that more hung on the presence
Of all the natural preoccupations,
Duties, emotions, daily obligations
Affections and responses than he'd guessed,
They'd grown a burden to him, but as a mother
Is burdened by her child's head when her breasts
Are thin and milkless; he knew this awful hanging
Obscene with urine, sagging on a limb,
Was not the end of life, and improved nothing.

Alun Lewis

ON A MEXICAN STRAW CHRIST

This is not the event. This
Is a man of straw,
The legs straw-thin
The straw-arms shent
And nailed. And yet this dry
Essence of agony must be
Close-grained to the one
They lifted down, when
Consummatum est the event was done.
Below the baroque straw—
Haloed basket-head
And the crown, far more
Like a cap, woven
For a matador than a crown of thorns,
A gap recedes: it makes
A mouth-in-pain, the teeth
Within it sideways-slashed
And gritted grin, are
Verticals of straw, and they
Emerge where the mask's
Chin ceases and become
Parallels plunging down, their sum
The body of God. Beneath,
Two feet join in one
Cramped culmination, as if
To say: 'I am the un-
Resurrection and the Death.'

Charles Tomlinson

GOOD FRIDAY

Three o'clock. The bus lurches
round into the sun: 'D's this go' –
he flops beside me – 'right along Bath Street?
– Oh tha's, tha's all right, see I've
got to get some Easter eggs for the kiddies.
I've had a wee drink, ye understand –
ye'll maybe think it's a funny day
to be celebratin' – well, no, but ye see
I wasny workin' – I don't say it's right,
I'm no sayin it's right, ye understand – ye understand?
I'm no lovin' ye, eh? ye see today,
I'm no borin' ye, eh? – ye see today,
But anyway tha's the way I look at it—
take today, I don't know what today is in aid of,
whether Christ was – crucified or was he –
rose frae the dead like, see what I mean?
You're an educatit man, you can tell me—
– Aye, well. There ye are. It's been seen
time and again, the workin' man
has nae education, he jist canny – jist
hasny got it, know what I mean,
he's jist bliddy ignorant – Christ aye,
bliddy ignorant. Well —' The bus brakes violently,
he lunges for the stairs, swings down – off,
into the sun for his Easter eggs,
on very nearly steady legs.

Edwin Morgan

GOOD FRIDAY NIGHT

Now lies the Lord in a most quiet bed.
  Stillness profound
Steeps like a balm the wounded body wholly,
More still than the hushed night brooding around.
  The moon is overhead,
Sparkling and small, and somewhere a faint sound
Of water dropping in a cistern slowly.
Now lies the Lord in a most quiet bed.

Now rests the Lord in perfect loneliness.
One little grated window has his tomb,
  A patch of gloom
Impenetrable, where the moonbeams whiten
  And arabesque its wall
With leafy shadows, light as a caress.
The palms that brood above the garden brighten,
  But in that quiet room
Darkness prevails, deep darkness fills it all.
Now rests the Lord in perfect loneliness.

Now sleeps the Lord secure from human sorrow.
The sorrowing women sometimes fall asleep
  Wrapped in their hair,
Which while they slumber yet warm tears will steep,
Because their hearts mourn in them ceaselessly.
  Uprising, half aware,
They myrrh and spices and rich balms put by
For their own burials, gather hastily,
  Dreaming it is that morrow
When they the precious body may prepare.
Now sleeps the Lord secure from human sorrow.

Now sleeps the Lord unhurt by love's betrayal.
  Peter sleeps not,
He lies yet on his face and has not stirred
Since the iron entered in his soul red-hot.
The disciples trembling mourn their disillusion,

That He whose word
Could raise the dead, on whom God had conferred
Power, as they trusted, to redeem Israel,
Had been that bitter day put to confusion,
    Crucified and interred.
Now sleeps the Lord unhurt by love's betrayal.

Now rests the Lord, crowned with ineffable peace.
Have they not peace tonight who feared Him, hated
    And hounded to his doom,
The red thirst of their vengeance being sated?
No, they still run about and bite the beard,
    Confer, nor cease
To tease the contemptuous Pilate, are affeared
Still of Him tortured, crushed, humiliated,
    Cold in a blood-stained tomb.
Now rests the Lord, crowned with ineffable peace.

Now lies the Lord, serene, august, apart,
That mortal life His mother gave Him ended.
    No word save one
Or Mary more, but gently as a cloud
On her perdurable silence has descended.
    Hush! in her heart
Which first felt the faint life stir in her son,
    Perchance is apprehended
Even now new mystery, grief less loud
Clamours, the Resurrection has begun.
Now lies the Lord serene, august, apart.

Margaret Louisa Woods

OH DEATH WHERE IS THY STING?

from RESURRECTION

The tomb, the tomb, that
Was her core and care, her one sore.
The light had hardly scarleted the dark
Or the first bird sung when Mary came in sight
With eager feet. Grief, like last night's frost,
Whitened her face and tightened all her tears.
It was there, then, there at the blinding turn
Of the bare future that she met her past.
She only heard his Angel tell her how
The holding stone broke open and gave birth
To her dear Lord, and how his shadow ran
To meet him like a dog.
And as the sun
Burns through the simmering muslins of the mist
Slowly his darkened voice, that seemed like doubt,
Morninged into noon; the summering bees
Mounted and boiled over in the bell-flowers.
'Come out of your jail, Mary,' he said, 'the doors are open
And joy has its ear cocked for your coming.
Earth now is no place to mope in. So throw away
Your doubt, cast every clout of care,
Hang all your hallelujahs out
This airy day.'

W. R. Rodgers

EASTER FOLK-SONG

To hear a far cock crowing
At midnight is not well:
When up and crew the black cock,
The demon plumed with hell,
The night before Good Friday
Great tears from Peter fell.

Its malice and its gloating
Went through him like a sword
Recalling how the third time
He had denied his Lord.

But the cock of Easter Sunday
Crowing at first light,
The white cock plumed with heaven,
Gold sheen among the white,
Sets every bell-throat singing
And heart's bell with delight.

But none sang more than Peter's,
Who knew so well, so well
His risen Lord forgave him
And the black cock down in hell.

Geoffrey Johnson

WORDS FOR A RESURRECTION

Each pale Christ stirring underground
Splits the brown casket of its root,
Wherefrom the rousing soil upthrusts
A narrow, pointed shoot.

And bones long quiet under frost
Rejoice as bells precipitate
The loud, ecstatic sundering,
The hour inviolate.

This Man of April walks again—
Such marvel does the time allow—
With laughter in His blessed bones,
And lilies on His brow.

Leo Kennedy

THE RESURRECTION

I was the one who waited in the garden
Doubting the morning and the early light.
I watched the mist lift off its own soft burden,
Permitting not believing my own sight.

If there were sudden noises I dismissed
Them as a trick of sound, a sleight of hand.
Not by a natural joy could I be blessed
Or trust a thing I could not understand.

Maybe I was a shadow thrown by one
Who, weeping, came to lift away the stone,
Or was I but the path on which the sun,
Too heavy for itself, was loosed and thrown?

I heard the voices and the recognition
And love like kisses heard behind thin walls.
Were they my tears which fell, a real contrition?
Or simply April with its waterfalls?

It was by negatives I learned my place.
The garden went on growing and I sensed
A sudden breeze that blew across my face.
Despair returned, but now it danced, it danced.

Elizabeth Jennings

SEEK AND YE SHALL FIND

from MOON'S FARM

A Dialogue for Three Voices

THIRD VOICE
You did not try
  to find your lost God?
SECOND VOICE
No. If God is still alive
  he is with us now
staring us in the face
His face is the sky
His eyes are red berries in yon hedge
  or the glittering quartz in this stone.
His voice is that bird
  crying in the gorse bush
  or the water
  lapping over the pebbles in the beck.
If God exists
  he must be both immanent and ubiquitous
What sort of God would play hide-and-seek?
THIRD VOICE
It takes two to play such a game.
SECOND VOICE
Yes: man is just as necessary to God
  as God to man.
God depends for his existence
  on our recognition of Him.
God is reborn
  in every woman's womb.

Herbert Read

THE INDIAN UPON GOD

I passed along the water's edge below the humid trees,
My spirit rocked in evening light, the rushes round my knees,
My spirit rocked in sleep and sighs; and saw the moorfowl pace
All dripping on a grassy slope, and saw them cease to chase
Each other round in circles, and heard the eldest speak:
Who holds the world between His bill and made us strong or weak
Is an undying moorfowl, and He lives beyond the sky.
The rains are from His dripping wing, the moonbeams from His eye.
I passed a little further on and heard a lotus talk:
Who made the world and ruleth it, He hangeth on a stalk,
For I am in His image made, and all this tinkling tide
Is but a sliding drop of rain between His petals wide.
A little way within the gloom a roebuck raised his eyes
Brimful of starlight, and he said: *The Stamper of the Skies,*
He is a gentle roebuck; for how else, I pray, could He
Conceive a thing so sad and soft, a gentle thing like me?
I passed a little further on and heard a peacock say:
Who made the grass and made the worms and made my feathers gay,
He is a monstrous peacock, and He waveth all the night
His languid tail above us, lit with myriad spots of light.

W. B. Yeats

THE THEOLOGY OF BONGWI, THE BABOON

This is the wisdom of the Ape
  Who yelps beneath the Moon—
'Tis God who made me in His shape
  He is a Great Baboon.
'Tis He who tilts the moon askew
  And fans the forest trees,
The heavens which are broad and blue
  Provide Him His trapeze;
He swings with tail divinely bent
  Around those azure bars
And munches to his Soul's content
  The kernels of the stars;
And when I die, His loving care
  Will raise me from the sod
To learn the perfect Mischief there,
  The Nimbleness of God.

Roy Campbell

HEAVEN

Fish (fly-replete in depth of June,
Dawdling away their wat'ry noon)
Ponder deep wisdom, dark or clear,
Each secret fishy hope or fear.
Fish say, they have their Stream or Pond;
But is there anything Beyond?
This life cannot be All, they swear,
Or how unpleasant, if it were!
One may not doubt that, somehow, Good
Shall come of Water and of Mud;
And sure, the reverent eye must see
A Purpose in Liquidity.
We darkly know, by Faith we cry,
The future is not Wholly Dry.
Mud unto mud!– Death eddies near—
Not here the appointed End, not here!
But somewhere, beyond Space and Time,
Is wetter water, slimier slime!
And there (they trust) there swimmeth One
Who swam ere rivers were begun,
Immense, of fishy form and mind,
Squamous, omnipotent, and kind;
And under that Almighty Fin,
The little fish may enter in.
Oh! never fly conceals a hook,
Fish say, in the Eternal Brook,
But more than mundane weeds are there,
And mud, celestially fair;
Fat caterpillars drift around,
And Paradisal grubs are found;
Unfading moths, immortal flies,
And the worm that never dies.
And in that Heaven of all their wish,
There shall be no more land, say fish.

Rupert Brooke

AND BECAUSE

A star shines in the sky. He follows you. When you move he moves.

(Dictionary compiled by six-year-olds.)

and because we listened

and listened not only among the incense and chanting
not only at premises of licensed amusement
not only in dreams or to the wisdom of actuaries
but listened also to the wind when we were lost in the mountains
listened in Petticoat Land
or listened to silence and a heartbeat after the dawn

a word was spoken

and because we looked

and looked not only among the tinsel and holly
not only at neon bottles for Magog
not only at paper lanterns and the full moon

but looked over the sea to the west at sunset
looked also at the Auroral ballet
or looked at a glowworm and the light of word

a star shone in the sky

and because we walked

and walked not only along paved cloisters
not only to the holy cities of seven religions
not only by fieldpaths or Fleet Street

but walked also from Tolpuddle Hiroshima Sophiatown
walked awake and sleeping
or walked the King's Road as far as the World's Beginning

the star came with us

and because the hotel was booked up for Christmas
we were boarded out with a girl who was nursing her baby

and the star stopped with us

and the next day we continued our journey.

John Knight

CHRIST IN THE CLAY-PIT

Why should I find Him here
And not in a church, nor yet
Where Nature heaves a breast like Olivet
Against the stars? I peer
Upon His footsteps in this quarried mud;
I see His blood
In rusty stains on pit-props, wagon-frames
Bristling with nails, not leaves: There were no leaves
Upon His chosen Tree,
No parasitic flowering over shames
Of Eden's primal infidelity.

Just splintered wood and nails
Were fairest blossoming for Him Who speaks
Where mica-silt outbreaks
Like water from the side of His own clay
In that strange day
When He was pierced. Here still the earth-face pales
And rends in earthquake roarings of a blast
With tainted rock outcast

While fields and woods lie dreaming yet of peace
'Twix God and His creation, of release
From potent wrath – a faith that waxes bold
In churches nestling snugly in the fold
Of scented hillsides where mild shadows brood.
The dark and stubborn mood
Of Him Whose feet are bare upon this mire,
And in the furnace fire
Which hardens all the clay that has escaped,
Would not be understood
By worshippers of beauty toned and shaped
To flower or hymn. I know their facile praise
False to the heart of me, which like this pit
Must still be disembowelled of Nature's stain,
And rendered fit
By violent mouldings through the tunnelled ways
Of all He would regain.

Jack Clemo

CHRIST IN WOOLWORTHS

I did not think to find you there—
Crucifixes, large and small,
Sixpence and threepence, on a tray,
Among the artificial pearls,
Paste rings, tin watches, beads of glass.
It seemed so strange to find you there
Fingered by people coarse and crass,
Who had no reverence at all.
Yet – What is it you would say?
'For these I hang upon my cross,
For these the agony and loss,
Though heedlessly they pass Me by.'
Dear Lord, forgive such fools as I
Who thought it strange to find you there
When you are with us everywhere.

Teresa Hooley

THE YOUNG MAN

There is a young man,
who lives in a world of progress.
He used to worship a God
who was kind to him.
This God had a long white beard,
He lived in the clouds,
but all the same
He was close to the solemn child
who had secretly
shut Him up, in a picture book.

But now,
the man is enlightened.
Now he has been to school,
and has learned to kick a ball,
and to be abject
in the face of public opinion.
He knows too,
that men are hardly removed from monkeys.
You see, he lives in the light
of the twentieth century.

He works, twelve hours a day,
and is able to rent a room,
in a lodging house,
that is not a home.
At night he hangs
a wretched coat
up on a peg on the door,
and stares
at the awful jug and basin,
and goes to bed.
And the poor coat,
worn to the man's shape,
round-shouldered and abject,
watches him, asleep,
dreaming of all
the essential
holy things,
that he cannot hope to obtain
for two pounds ten a week.

Very soon
he will put off his body,
like the dejected coat
that he hates.
And his body will be
worn to the shape
of twelve hours' work a day
for two pounds ten a week.

If he had only known
that the God in the picture book,
is not an old man in the clouds
but the seed of life in his soul,
the man would have lived.
And his life would have flowered
with the flower of limitless joy.

But he does not know,
and in him
the Holy Ghost
is a poor little bird
in a cage,
who never sings,
and never opens his wings,
yet never, never
desires to be gone away.

Caryll Houselander

IN A COUNTRY CHURCH

To one kneeling down no word came,
Only the wind's song, saddening the lips
Of the grave saints, rigid in glass;
Or the dry whisper of unseen wings,
Bats not angels, in the high roof.

Was he balked by silence? He kneeled long,
And saw love in a dark crown
Of thorns blazing, and a winter tree
Golden with fruit of a man's body.

R. S. Thomas

IMMANENCE

I come in little things,
Saith the Lord:
Not borne on morning wings
Of majesty, but I have set My feet
Amidst the delicate and bladed wheat
That springs triumphant in the furrowed sod.
There do I dwell, in weakness and in power;
Not broken or divided, saith our God!
In your strait garden plot I come to flower:
About your porch My Vine
Meek, fruitful, doth entwine;
Waits, at the threshold, Love's appointed hour.

I come in little things,
Saith the Lord:
Yea! on the glancing wings
Of eager birds, the softly pattering feet
Of furred and gentle beasts, I come to meet
Your hard and wayward hearts. In brown, bright eyes
That peep from out the brake I stand confest.
On every nest
Where feathery Patience is content to brood
And leaves her pleasure for the high emprize
Of motherhood—
There doth My Godhead rest.

I come in little things,
Saith the Lord:
My starry wings
I do forsake
Love's highway of humility to take:
Meekly I fit my stature to your need.
In beggar's part
About your gates I shall not cease to plead—
As man, to speak with man —
Till by such art
I shall achieve My Immemorial Plan
Pass the low lintel of the human heart.

Evelyn Underhill

THE JUNK MAN

I am glad God saw Death
And gave Death a job taking care of all who are tired of living:
When all the wheels in a clock are worn and slow and the
   connections loose,
And the clock goes on ticking and telling the wrong time from
   hour to hour
And people around the house joke about what a bum clock it is.
How glad the clock is when the big Junk Man drives his wagon
Up to the house and puts his arms round the clock and says:
   'You don't belong here,
   You gotta come
   Along with me,'
How glad the clock is then, when it feels the arms of the Junk
   Man close around it and carry it away.

Carl Sandburg

ON THE SWAG

His body doubled
  under the pack
  that sprawled untidily
  on his old back,
  the cold wet deadbeat
  plods up the track.

The cook peers out:
  'O curse that old lag
  here again
  with his clumsy swag
  made of a dirty
  old turnip bag.'

'Bring him in, cook,
  from the grey level sleet,
  put silk on his body,
  slippers on his feet,
  give him fire
  and bread and meat.

Let the fruit be plucked
  and the cake be iced,
  and the bed be snug
  and the wine be spiced
  in the old cove's nightcap:
  for this is Christ.'

R. A. K. Mason

GOD ABIDES IN MEN

God abides in men,
Because Christ has put on
the nature of man, like a garment,
and worn it to His own shape.
He has put on everyone's life.
He has fitted Himself to the little child's dress,
to the shepherd's coat of sheepskin,
to the workman's coat,
to the King's red robes,
to the snowy loveliness of the wedding garment,
and to the drab
of the sad, simple battle dress.

Christ has put on man's nature,
and given him back his humanness,
worn to the shape
of limitless love,
and warm from the touch
of His life.

He has given man His crown,
the thorn that is jewelled
with drops of His blood.
He has given him
the seamless garment
of His truth.
He has bound him
in the swaddling bands
of His humility.
He has fastened his hands
to the tree of life.

He has latched his feet
in crimson sandals
that they move not
from the path of love.

God abides in man.

Caryll Houselander

TO THE SUN

O let your shining orb grow dim,
Of Christ the mirror and the shield,
That I may gaze through you to Him,
See half the miracle revealed,
And in your seven hues behold
The Blue Man walking on the sea;
The Green, beneath the summer tree,
Who called the children; then the Gold,
with palms; the Orange, flaring bold
with scourges; Purple in the garden
(As Greco saw); and then the Red
Torero (Him who took the toss
And rode the black horns of the cross—
But rose snow-silver from the dead!)

Roy Campbell

OMEGA

First—
How shall I pen my O
Gaily to make it show
A hoop a wheel a merry-go-round,
Sound in a whirl of music bound,
How shall I round my O?

Next—
How shall I pen my O
Proudly to make it show
A moon a planet circle in dance
The O of the sun's great countenance,
How shall I swell my O?

Last —
How shall I pen my O
Perfect to make it show
A closed, yet an eternal, ring,
A nothing, something, everything?
I cannot end my O.
Tu
Jesu parvule,
Matris in gremio
Alpha
es et
O.

George Rostrevor Hamilton

BABYLON THE GREAT IS FALLEN

from FIGURES FOR AN APOCALYPSE

Landscape: Beast
Yonder, by the eastward sea
Where smoke melts in a saucer of extinguished cities,
The last men stand, in delegations,
Waiting to see the seven-headed business
Promised us, from those unpublished deeps:
Waiting to see those horns and diadems
And hear the seven voices of the final blasphemy.

And westward, where the other waters are as slick as silk
And slide, in the grey evening, with uncertain lights,
(Screened by the smoke of the extinguished studios)
The last men wait to see the seven-headed thing.
They stand round the radios
Wearing their regalia on their thin excited breasts,
Waving the signal of their masonry.
What will happen, when they see those heads, those horns
Dishevel the flickering sea?
How will they bear their foreheads, and put forth their hands
And wince with the last indelible brand,
And wear the dolour of that animal's number,
And evermore be burned with her disgusting name?

Inland, in the lazy distance, where a dozen planes still play
As loud as horseflies, round the ruins of an average town,
A blue-green medium dragon, swimming in the river,
Emerges from the muddy waters, comes to romp awhile upon the
    land.
She rises on the pathless shore,
And goes to roll in the ashes of the ravaged country.
But no man turns to see and be surprised
Where those grey flanks flash palely in the sun.
Who shall gather to see an ordinary dragon, in this day of anger,
Or wonder at those scales as usual as sin?

Meanwhile, upon the broken mountains of the south
No one observes the angels passing to and fro:

And no one sees the fire that shoots beneath the hoofs
Of all the white, impatient horses.

And no one hears or fears the music of those blazing swords.

(Northward, northward, what lies there to see?
Who shall recount the terror of those ruined streets?
And who shall dare to look where all the birds with golden beaks

Stab at the blue eyes of the murdered saints?)

Thomas Merton

AND I SAW A NEW HEAVEN
AND A NEW EARTH

from THE ROCK

We build in vain unless the LORD build with us.
Can you keep the city that the LORD keeps not with you?
A thousand policemen directing the traffic
Cannot tell you why you come or where you go.
A colony of cavies or a hoard of active marmots
Build better than they who build without the LORD.
Shall we lift up our feet among perpetual ruins?
I have loved the beauty of Thy House, the peace of Thy sanctuary,
I have swept the floors and garnished the altars.
Where there is no temple there shall be no homes,
Though you have shelters and institutions,
Precarious lodgings while the rent is paid,
Subsiding basements where the rat breeds
Or sanitary dwellings with numbered doors
Or a house a little better than your neighbour's;
When the Stranger says: 'What is the meaning of this city?
Do you huddle close together because you love each other?'
What will you answer? 'We all dwell together
To make money from each other'? or 'This is a community'?
And the Stranger will depart and return to the desert.
O my soul, be prepared for the coming of the Stranger,
Be prepared for him who knows how to ask questions.

O weariness of men who turn from GOD
To the grandeur of your mind and the glory of your action,
To arts and inventions and daring enterprises,
To schemes of human greatness thoroughly discredited,
Binding the earth and the water to your service,
Exploiting the seas and developing the mountains,
Dividing the stars into common and preferred,
Engaged in devising the perfect refrigerator,
Engaged in working out a rational morality,
Engaged in printing as many books as possible,
Plotting of happiness and flinging empty bottles,
Turning from your vacancy to fevered enthusiasm
For nation or race or what you call humanity;

AND I SAW A NEW HEAVEN AND A NEW EARTH

Though you forget the way to the Temple,
There is one who remembers the way to your door:
Life you may evade, but Death you shall not.
You shall not deny the Stranger.

T. S. Eliot

BRIEF BIOGRAPHICAL NOTES ON POETS

ANDERSON, John Redwood (1883–1963)
Born in Manchester; educated privately and for a short time at Oxford. Assistant schoolmaster 1915–43. Has published a number of volumes of poetry.
Before Ararat (Genesis **8.**9) . . . . page 46

AUDEN, Wystan Hugh (1907–)
Born at York and educated at Oxford. Leader of group of 'Left Wing' poets in the 1930s. Wrote poetic drama with Christopher Isherwood. Stretcher-bearer on Republican side in Spanish Civil War. Has been schoolmaster in England and Scotland. Went to U.S.A. 1938 and became a naturalized American. Professor of English at Ann Arbor University, Michigan. Professor of Poetry at Oxford. Notable for the free vigour of his verse.
The Sabbath . . . . . . page 25

BLACKBURN, Thomas (1916–)
Born in Cumberland. Gregory Fellow of Poetry at Leeds University 1956–8. Now Principal Lecturer in English at the College of St. Mark and St. John, Chelsea. *The Judas Tree* is part of a musical drama.
The Judas Tree . . . . . . page 102

BOWEN, Arthur Vincent (1901–47)
Born and educated in Calcutta. Came to England 1922. Teacher and actor. Joined regular army 1928. Active service 1939. Invalided out of army 1944. Lecturer, poet, writer.
In Eden (Genesis **2.**17) . . . . . page 29

BROOKE, Rupert (1877–1915)
Born at Rugby. Father a housemaster at Rugby School, where the poet was educated before he went up to Cambridge. Travelled in Europe and round the world. When First World War broke out he joined the army. Was sent to the Mediterranean in 1915. He died and was buried at Skyros on 23 April that year. A poet of exceptional promise.
Heaven . . . . . . page 119

CAMPBELL, Roy (1901–57)
Born in Durban. Educated at Natal University. A poet and a man of action. Fought in Spanish War on side of Franco, and during 1939–45 in North and East Africa. Lived in France, Spain and Portugal. An accomplished bull-fighter. Talks producer with B.B.C.
from *The Flaming Terrapin* (Genesis 7. 18) . . . page 40
The Theology of Bongwi, the Baboon . . . page 118
To the sun . . . . . . page 131

Causley, Charles (1917–)
Born at Launceston, Cornwall, where he still lives. Writer, poet, editor, teacher. Served in Royal Navy 1940–6. Has edited an anthology of modern verse for children and a selection of twentieth-century ballads.
The Ballad of the Bread Man . . . . page 81

Chesterton, Gilbert Keith (1874–1936)
Born in London. Went to St. Paul's School and then studied art at the Slade. Gave that up to work in a publisher's office, and left to become a journalist. From 1905–30 wrote an essay a week for *Illustrated London News*. Wrote novels, essays, plays, biographies, histories, detective stories and poetry. Perhaps his best-known writings are the *Father Brown stories*.
On Righteous Indignation (Genesis 3.24) . . . page 36

Clemo, Reginald Jack (1916–)
Born in Cornwall and educated at Trenthosa Council School, St. Austell. In 1948 he won the Atlantic Award from Birmingham University for a novel; also the Arts Council Festival Prize. Has published novels and poetry. Blind and deaf since an early age.
Christ in the Clay Pit . . . . page 121

Cullen, Countee (1903–46)
Negro poet. Educated New York University and Harvard. His poems have been published in various magazines. Edited an anthology of Negro verse in 1927, and published a novel, *One Way to Heaven*, 1932.
Simon the Cyrenian Speaks (Matthew 27.32;
    Mark 15.21; Luke 23.26) . . . page 95

Dearmer, Geoffrey (1893–)
Born in London. Educated Westminster School and Oxford. Examiner of plays to the Lord Chamberlain and editor of Children's Hour Department of the B.B.C. Has published novels, plays, poetry.
Epstein's Madonna and Child . . . page 68

Eliot, Thomas Stearns (1888–1965)
Of American birth. Educated Harvard, Sorbonne and Oxford. Came to London 1913 and in 1927 became naturalized British. Worked in bank and as schoolmaster. Director of publishing firm. His free verse forms and vigorous writing have exercised a profound influence on younger poets. His chief works are: *The Waste Land, Ash Wednesday, Murder in the Cathedral, The Four Quartets.*
A Song for Simeon (Luke 2.25) . . . page 62
Journey of the Magi (Matthew 2.1) . . . page 60
from *The Rock* . . . . . page 138

Fry, Christopher (1907–)
Educated at Bedford Modern School. Earned his living as a schoolmaster, actor, director of theatres, and dramatist. Awarded Queen's Gold Medal for poetry 1962. Has written many well-known plays: *The Lady's not for Burning, The Firstborn*, etc. Wrote film commentary for *The Queen is Crowned* (the coronation of Queen Elizabeth II) and part of the film scripts for *Ben Hur, The Bible*, and *Barabbas*.
from *The Firstborn* (Exodus 12.3) . . . page 52

GASCOYNE, David (1916–)
Born in Harrow and went to school in the Close at Salisbury. Was a chorister in the Cathedral Choir for six years. For six years before the war he lived in Paris. During the war he was a ship's cook and acted for ENSA. His first poems were printed in his school magazine.

GLYN, Susan (1923–)
Brought up in Wales. Did not go to school. Served in the war as an anti-aircraft gunner. Qualified after marriage as a barrister. Studied philosophy as an external student of London University. Wife of novelist Antony Glyn. Is well-known as an artist specializing in abstract religious paintings. At present living in Paris.

GOGARTY, Oliver St. John (1878–1957)
Educated Stoneyhurst and Trinity College, Dublin. Senator of Irish Free State 1922–36. Doctor, athlete, airman, poet, novelist. Friend of AE (George Russell) and of W. B. Yeats. Collected poems published 1952. Autobiography: *As I Was Going Down Sackville Street.*

GRAVES, Robert (1895–)
Born in London of mixed Irish, Scottish, Danish and German parentage. Educated Charterhouse and Oxford. Served in France 1914–18. Professor of Language and Literature at Oxford. Now lives in Majorca.

GUNN, Thom (1929–)
Born in Kent and educated at Cambridge and Stanford University, California. In 1959 received the Somerset Maugham Award. Has published several books of poems. Now lives in America.

HAMILTON, Sir George Rostrevor (1888–1967)
Educated at Oxford: first-class degree in Honour Mods. and in Greats. Presiding Special Commissioner of Income Tax 1950–3. Knighted 1951. Poet and critic.

HARTNOLL, Phyllis (1906–)
Educated at Oxford. Gained Newdigate Prize for poetry 1929. Has published several volumes of poems.

HESKETH, Phoebe (1909–)
Educated Cheltenham College. Worked on northern newspaper for two years. Awarded Greenwood Prize of the Poetry Society 1946.

HEATH-STUBBS, John (1918–)
Read English at Oxford. Has worked as private tutor, schoolmaster and in the publishing business. Was Visiting Professor of English at Alexandria University and at Michigan University. Has written articles on Augustan, Romantic and Modern poetry.

L

HODGSON, Ralph (1871–1967)
Born in Yorkshire. Worked as journalist in Fleet Street. In 1924 appointed lecturer in English literature at Sendai University, Japan. Lived in America. A man of letters and also a leading authority on bull terriers.

HOOLEY, Teresa (1888–)
Born Risley, Derbyshire. Educated privately, started to write at eighteen years of age and has published some twelve books. Has contributed to many anthologies in England and America. Many of her poems have been broadcast; she has appeared on television. Main interests, apart from poetry, are nature and reading.

HOUSELANDER, Caryll (1901–54)
Born in Bath and educated at the Convent School, Olton (France) and at St. Johns Wood Art School. Worked as a painter. Was an active social worker for the Catholic Church in the East End of London. Approach to Christianity that of a mystic. Probably the best-known Catholic poet of modern times.

HOUSMAN, Alfred Edward (1859–1936)
Born in Shropshire. Educated at Oxford. Distinguished classical scholar. Professor of Latin at London and Cambridge. Editor and poet. Wrote numerous articles in classical journals. Perhaps his best-known work is The Shropshire Lad, 1896.

JENNINGS, Elizabeth (1926–)
Born Boston. Educated Oxford. Assistant Librarian in Oxford City Library 1950–8. Worked as editorial assistant for publishing firm. Now devotes full time to writing. Has been awarded an Arts Council Prize and the Somerset Maugham Award. Poet, editor, critic. Translated Michelangelo's sonnets. Has written a book entitled Christianity and Poetry.

JOHNSON, Geoffrey (1900–1967)
Born in the Black Country. Educated at London University. Taught in a grammar school

JOHNSON, James Weldon (1871–1938)
Negro author, born in Florida, educated Atlanta and Columbia. Teacher and lawyer. Collaborated with his brother John Rosamond Johnson in writing songs and light opera. Became a well-known writer and lecturer; active in various Negro reform groups. Works include: God's Trombones, studies of Negro life, and his autobiography, Along this Way.

JOSEPH, Michael Kennedy (1914–)
Born in Essex and educated at the Sacred Heart College, Auckland, Auckland University and Oxford. Lecturer in English at Auckland University College; Associate Professor, 1960.
The New Moses (Exodus **13**.21) . . . . page 56

KENNEDY, Leo (1907–)
Born in Liverpool and taken to Canada at the age of five years. Educated at Montreal. Associated with Canadian literary reviews. Lives in the U.S.A. and works as an advertising writer. In 1933 published a collection of poems: *The Shrouding*.
Words for a Resurrection . . . . . page 113

KEYES, Sidney (1922–43)
One of the most promising of the young poets killed during the Second World War. His poetry displays a delightful originality. Born in Kent and educated at Oxford. Died during the last days of the campaign in Tunisia after only a fortnight's active service. Posthumously awarded Hawthornden Prize. *Collected Poems* 1945.
St. John Baptist (Matthew **3**.1; Mark **1**.4;
Luke **3**.3; John **1**.15) . . . . . page 72

KIRKUP, James (1912–)
Born at South Shields, Co. Durham. Educated at King's College, Newcastle-on-Tyne. Won the Atlantic Award in Literature in 1950. Was first holder of the Gregory Fellowship in Poetry at Leeds University. Visiting Poet at Bath Academy of Arts 1953–6. Professor of English at Salamanca, at Tohoku University, Japan 1958–61. Now lives in Tokyo, where he works as a literary editor. Served as a conscientious objector in various prisons and labour camps during the Second World War. Is a pacifist. Poet, novelist, dramatist, he was recently elected Fellow of the Royal Society of Literature.
Cena (Matthew **26**.20; Mark **14**.18;
Luke **22**.14.) . . . . . page 89

KNIGHT, John (1906–)
Spent his childhood in Cornwall. Since 1932 has worked in industrial Lancashire and Yorkshire. Began writing poems as a child, but most of his best poems have been written since 1957.
Father to the Man . . . . . page 98
And Because . . . . . page 120

LARKIN, Philip (1922–)
Educated at Oxford. Has published a novel and two collections of poems. Librarian to the University of Hull.
Church Going . . . . . page 12

LAWRENCE, David Herbert (1885–1930)
The son of a miner, born in Nottinghamshire. Educated at University College, Nottingham. Started to teach, but later devoted himself to writing. Travelled widely in Italy, New Mexico and Australia. Is buried in Vence, in the south of France, where his grave is marked by a phoenix carved in stone. One of the great novelists and poets of the twentieth century.
Only Man . . . . . page 37

LEWIS, Alun (1918–44)
Born in a welsh mining village. Educated at Oxford and became a school-master. Served in the Second World War. Wrote poetry, letters and short stories. Died in an accident in 1944.

LEWIS, Clive Staples (1898–)
Educated at Oxford, where he took a first in Greats and in English. Served as 2nd Lieutenant during 1917–19. Became a university lecturer and professor of English. Awarded Hawthornden Prize for Poetry 1936; and the Library Association Carnegie Medal in 1957. He is a critic, a writer of religious works, a children's author as well as a poet. His publications include: *Problem of Pain*, and *The Screwtape Letters*.

MASON, Ronald Allison Kells (1905–)
Born in Auckland and educated at Auckland University College. Writes novels, critical works, poetry, radio plays.

MacNEICE, Louis (1907–63)
Born in Belfast, son of the Bishop of Down, Connor and Dromore. Educated at Marlborough and Oxford. Lecturer in Classics at Birmingham University 1930; Lecturer in Greek at Bedford College, London. Worked for B.B.C. from 1941 and wrote radio plays and feature programmes. Published five volumes of poetry; travel books, poetic drama, and a collection of radio plays. One of the leading poets of the 1930s.

MERTON, Thomas (1915–)
Born in France and educated in France, England and America. Taught English at various universities before entering the Trappist Monastery in 1941. Ordained priest 1949. His more than twenty volumes, which include his autobiography *Elected Silence*, have been translated into at least nine languages.

MONRO, Harold (1879–1932)
Educated at Cambridge. Travelled widely. Started The Poetry Book Shop and sold the first works of little-known poets. A Londoner who wrote about the country from the viewpoint of a loving weekender.

MORGAN, Edwin (1920–)
Born in Glasgow and is a lecturer in English at Glasgow University. His poems and translations have appeared in many anthologies.

MUIR, Edwin (1887–)
Born in the Orkney Islands. At fourteen years of age was a clerk in a ship-building firm in Glasgow. Published work as a poet, critic, journalist, novelist and translator.

NICHOLS, Robert (1893–1944)
Born in Essex and educated at Oxford. Served in the army on the Western Front in the First World War. For a time he was Professor of English at the Imperial University, Tokyo.

NICHOLSON, Norman (1914–)
Born at Millom, Cumberland, and has always lived there. At Millom the traditional and the modern ways of life meet: industry and the countryside; factories and the seaside. In his poetry, Norman Nicholson seeks to interpret that impact.

POUND, Ezra (1885–)
Born in Idaho and educated at the University of Pennsylvania. Taught in Indiana. Came to Europe in 1908. Lived in Rapallo until he gave himself up to the American troops in 1944. He was arrested as an alleged traitor for his wartime broadcasts. He was imprisoned and declared insane. Author of many volumes of modernistic poetry, he was one of the founders of the Imagist Movement.

RAMSEY, Thomas Weston (1892–)
A Londoner, educated at London University. President of the Poetry Society 1948. Has published several volumes of poetry.

READ, Herbert (1893–)
Born in Yorkshire and educated at Leeds University. From 1922–31 he was Assistant Keeper at the Victoria and Albert Museum. Collected poems 1947. Autobiography, *The Innocent Eye*, published 1933.

RODGERS, William Robert (1909–)
Born in Belfast and educated at Queen's University, Belfast. Was a Presbyterian clergyman in Co. Armagh for twelve years. Resigned in 1946 and joined the B.B.C. Features Department. Has published several volumes of poetry and has written scripts for radio feature programmes. In 1951 he was elected to the Irish Academy of Letters.

SANDBURG, Carl (1878–)
Born in Illinois of Swedish immigrant parents. As a young man he earned his living working in hotel kitchens and in the wheat fields. Served for eight months with the army in the Puerto Rican campaigns, and then worked his way through college. Was organizer of the Social Democrat Party in Milwaukee, and was secretary to the Mayor. Journalist and editor, as well as poet and novelist; has written a biography of Lincoln.

SANSOM, Clive
Writer and lecturer: an authority on speech and speech training about which he has written several books. He has published poetry and has edited various anthologies. Lives in Reigate, Surrey.

Mary of Nazareth . . . . page 59
Martha of Bethany (Luke 10.38) . . . page 78
The Centurion (Matthew 27.33; Mark 15.22;
  Luke 23.27; John 19.17) . . . page 96
The Donkey's Owner (Matthew 21.2; Mark 11.2;
  Luke 19.30; John 12.14) . . . . page 84

SASSOON, Siegfried (1886–)
Educated at Cambridge. Served in France and Palestine in the First World War, and was awarded the M.C. One of the leading poets of the war; his poetry was a vigorous denunciation of the horrors of war.
  The Power and the Glory . . . . . page 22

SMITH, Stevie (1902–)
Born in Hull and educated at North London Collegiate School for Girls. Has worked in a publisher's office, and has written criticism for the leading daily papers. She has published several novels, poems and drawings.
  Oh Christianity, Christianity . . . . page 6

SPENDER, Stephen (1909–)
Educated at Oxford. Has travelled widely in Europe and lived for some time in Germany. Was in Spain during the Civil War. One of the leading poets of the 1930s.
  Judas Iscariot . . . . . . page 87

STEPHENS, James (1882–1951)
A Dubliner, who was discovered by AE (George Russell) working as a typist in a lawyer's office. Russell encouraged him to become a writer and poet. First verse published in 1909. Lived the last years of his life in London.
  In the Cool of the Evening (Genesis 3.8) . . . page 28

TAGORE, Sir Rabindranath (1861–1941)
Born in Calcutta and studied Law in England, but abandoned this for poetry. On the death of his father, he returned to India to manage the family estates. He founded a school in Bengal; was awarded the Nobel Prize in 1913, and was knighted in 1915.
  The Son of Man . . . . . . page 11

THOMAS, R. S. (1913–)
Born in Cardiff and became Rector of Manafon in 1942. His first volume of poetry, *The Stones of the Field,* was published in 1946. *An Acre of Land* was published in 1952. *The Minister* (1953) was written specially for broadcasting. He has contributed to various literary periodicals.
  In a Country Church . . . . page 126

TILLER, Terence (1916–)
Born in Cornwall and educated at Cambridge. Awarded the Chancellor's Medal for English Verse in 1936. Lectured in history at Cambridge 1937–9. Lecturer at Faud I University 1939–46. Worked for some time on verse programmes for B.B.C.
  from *A Hymn for Eve* (Genisis 2.25) . . . page 20
  Three Christmas Trees . . . . . page 65

TOMLINSON, Charles (1927–)
Born at Stoke on Trent and educated at Cambridge. Has held various academic posts, including that of lecturer at Bristol University, 1964. His poetry is characterized by a fusion of the abstract and the concrete, by the delicate

movement of the verse and by an assured diction. The world is a desolate but moral world. 'What one sees discovers what one is.'

On a Mexican Straw Christ . . . . . page 107

UNDERHILL, Evelyn (1825–1941)
Educated at King's College for Women, London. Studied history and botany. Interested in yachting and travel, especially in France and Italy. Began writing when she was sixteen and developed into an important religious writer. Became a convert to the Anglican Church 1921. During 1914–18 worked for Admiralty; 1939–45 was a Christian Pacifist. Her favourite saying was one of St. Teresa's: 'To give our Lord a perfect service, Mary and Martha must combine.'

Immanence . . . . . . page 126

WOODS, Margaret Louisa (1856–1929)
Born in Rugby, daughter of the Dean of Westminster. Wrote several novels, poems and plays. Her collected works were published in 1913.

Good Friday Night (Matthew 27.66; Mark 15.46;
    Luke 23.53; John 19.42) . . . . page 109

YEATS, William Butler (1865–1939)
Leading figure in Irish Literary Renaissance. Born and educated in Dublin. Art student for three years. Helped to found the Abbey Theatre. Senator of the Irish Free State 1922–8. Nobel Prize for literature 1923.

The Indian upon God . . . . . page 117

YOUNG, Andrew (1885–)
Born in Elgin; educated at Edinburgh University; now Vicar of Stonegate, Sussex and Canon of Chichester Cathedral. Used to play truant from school and even though he did not like the countryside, he was forced to seek refuge there. That was how he became interested in wild flowers!

from Nicodemus (John 2.23) . . . . page 90

LIST OF ILLUSTRATIONS WITH SHORT BIOGRAPHIES OF ARTISTS

Plate No. 1
Where do we come from? Who are we? Where are we going?
PAUL GAUGUIN
Gauguin was born in Paris in 1848 and was a friend of Pissarro, the French Impressionist. He lived part of his life in Panama and Martinique, and in his later years in Tahiti. The great allegory, *Where do we come from? Who are we? Where are we going?* was inspired by the death of his favourite child. He resolved to commit suicide when the painting was finished, and he took arsenic, but recovered. As a result of denouncing as corrupt the administration in the Marquesas Islands, where he was then living, he was found guilty of libel and sentenced to three months imprisonment, but died in 1903 before he could appeal against the sentence.

Plate No. 2
The Cosmos
FRANK J. MALINA
Born in Brenham, U.S.A. 1912, a scientist of international renown. Has exhibited structural reliefs in Europe and America. In 1965 while watching the construction of the new building of Pergamon Press, Ltd. at Headington, Oxford, he conceived the idea of the kinetic mural, *The Cosmos*, which might, he says, be called an expression of 'peaceful' cosmos. 'Man, that frail creature of earth dares to venture further and further away from his planetary cradle. The artist is challenged to find aesthetic significance in these experiences or mock them in despair.' Malina now lives in France.

Plate No. 3
Eve
ILSA RODMELL
Born in Illzach, a small village in Alsace, Ilsa Rodmell has always been interested in painting, but started serious work in oils only in her early forties. Inventiveness and originality have always been allowed full play in her work. The world of childhood and fantasy is reflected in her large-eyed figures. Human interests have always been important in her life; they are for her the true material of art. Ilsa Rodmell now lives in Brighton.

Plate No. 4
Noah's Ark
ELISABETH BAILLON
Has made a name in the world of art for her treatment of religious themes. Her tapestry *Noah's Ark* was displayed at the Contemporary Christian Art, Inc., New York.

Plate No. 5
Pharaoh's daughter finds Moses
ADA and EMILE NOLDE
Emile Nolde was a German painter and one of the leaders of the Expressionist movement in his own country. Influenced by Gauguin and by primitive art. He painted Biblical subjects with a vigorous, almost barbaric, intensity of colour. Denounced as a 'degenerate' in 1933. In 1941 was forbidden to paint.

Plate No. 6
The Annunciation
SUSAN GLYN
Born 1923, brought up in Wales and privately educated. Susan Glyn served in World War II as an AA gunner. She is married to Anthony Glyn, the novelist, has two daughters and is a qualified barrister. She is now studying philosophy as an extern student at London University. Both a poet and an artist, she specialises in abstract religious paintings. In *The Annunciation* she follows ecclesiastical tradition and makes a feature of brilliant rose madder againt a very dark blue violet.

Plate No. 7
Christ in the Wilderness – Foxes
STANLEY SPENCER
One of the greatest 20th century English painters. Born in Berkshire in 1891 and lived there for most of his life. Studied at the Slade School from 1910–1914. The two most important influences in his life were Cookham, the village where he was born, and the Bible. The importance of the latter can be seen in the wide range of Biblical subjects that he painted.

Plate No. 8
The Crucifixion
GRAHAM SUTHERLAND, O.M.
Born 1903 in London and educated at Goldsmith School of Art. Converted to Roman Catholicism in 1926. In 1949 he was appointed a Trustee of the Tate Gallery, and in 1952 he accepted the commission to design the great tapestry for the new Coventry Cathedral; the Coventry Tapestry was completed in 1962. In 1961–63 he painted *The Crucifixion* for the Catholic Church of St. Aidan, Acton. Awarded the Order of Merit in 1960.

Plate No. 9
Baptistry Window, Coventry Cathedral
JOHN PIPER
A painter and writer, born at Epsom, 1903. He painted water-colours and striking aquatints of architectural subjects. Did a series of water-colours for Windsor Castle at the request of H.M. the Queen. A Trustee of the Tate Gallery, 1946–53. Was commissioned to design the windows for Eton College Chapel and Nuffield College Chapel. The window in Coventry Cathedral, one of his greatest works, was completed in 1962.

Plate No. 10
Geopoliticus Child watches the birth of the New Man
SALVADOR DALI
Catalan painter, born in Figuras 1904. Expelled from Madrid Academy and settled in Paris. Interested in psycho-analysis and 'art nouveau'. His fantastic imagination is seen in his smoothly painted but often weird pictures.

Plate No. 11
The Church of Our Lady of Grace, Plateau d'Assy, France
Since the 1939–45 war an increasing number of modern artists have been engaged in the design and decoration of Catholic Churches; many of the artists are recognised masters in the world of contemporary art. The church at Assy is an outstanding example of their work.

FERNAND LÉGER (painter)
Born in Argentan in 1881. Became an architect's draughtsman in Paris. Studied painting and was influenced by Cubism and modern mechanical forms. His work includes book illustration, designs for wall decorations, mosaics and stained glass.

MAURICE NOVARINA (architect)
Born in 1917, a French architect who specialised in ecclesiastical architecture. Built the Church of the Sacred Heart at Audincourt and collaborated with Léger at Assy.

ACKNOWLEDGEMENTS

Acknowledgement is due to the following for permission to use copyright material:

Messrs. Faber and Faber Ltd. for *Sabbath* by W. H. AUDEN from *Homage to Clio*, *The Animals, Moses*, and *The Transfiguration* by EDWIN MUIR from *Collected Poems, Journey of the Magi, A Song for Simeon*, and extract from *The Rock*, by T. S. ELIOT. *The Burning Bush* from *Five Rivers* and *Innocents' Day* from *The Pot Geranium* by NORMAN NICHOLSON, *Judas Iscariot* by STEPHEN SPENDER from *The Edge of Being, Jesus and His Mother* from *Sense of Movement* and *Lazarus not Raised* from *Fighting Terms* by THOM GUNN, extract from *Autumn Journal* by LOUIS MACNEICE from *Collected Poems, Ballad of the Goodly Fere* by EZRA POUND from *Personae;* David Higham Associates Ltd. for *The Ballad of the Bread Man* by CHARLES CAUS-LEY which first appeared in *Poetry Review, Mary of Nazareth, Martha of Bethany, The Donkey's Owner, The Centurion* by CLIVE SANSOM from *The Witnesses and Other Poems*, extract from *Moon's Farm* by HERBERT READ from *Collected Poems, History of the Flood* by JOHN HEATH-STUBBS from *Selected Poems* published by Oxford University Press; The Marvell Press for *Church Going* by PHILIP LARKIN reprinted from *The Less Deceived;* Messrs. J. M. Dent and Sons Ltd. for *Immanence* by EVELYN UNDER-HILL, *Cena* by JAMES KIRKUP from *Paper Windows;* Messrs MacMillan and Co. Ltd. for *The Son of Man* from *The Fugitive and Other Poems* by RA-BINDRANATH TAGORE from *Collected Poems and Plays* of Rabindranath Tagore by permission of the Trustees of the Tagore Estate, *In the Cool of the Evening* by JAMES STEPHENS from the *Collected Poems* of James Stephens by permission of Mrs. Iris Wise, *Eve* by RALPH HODGSON from the *Collected Poems* of Ralph Hodgson by permission of Mrs. Hodgson; Messrs. George Allen and Unwin Ltd. for *The Creation* by WELDON JOHNSON from *God's Trombones, The Crucifixion* by ALUN LEWIS from *HA! HA! Among the Trumpets;* Oxford University Press for an extract from *The Firstborn* by CHRISTOPHER FRY, *Ecce Homo* by DAVID GASCOYNE from *Collected Poems, On a Mexican Straw Christ* by CHARLES TOMLINSON from *American Scenes;* Messrs. André Deutsch Ltd. for *Lazarus, The Resurrection, The Annunciation* by ELIZABETH JENNINGS; Messrs. Jonathan Cape Ltd. for an extract from *The Flaming Terrapin* by ROY CAMPBELL by permission of the executors of the Roy Campbell Estate, *Cabbages* by TERESA HOOLEY from *Selected Poems;* Messrs. Curtis Brown Ltd. for *The Theology of Bongwi the Baboon* by ROY CAMPBELL; Messrs. Chatto and Windus Ltd. for *The Tower* by ROBERT NICHOLS by permission of Mr. Milton Waldman; Messrs. Longmans Green and Co. Ltd. for *Oh Christianity, Christianity* by STEVIE SMITH from *The Frog Prince and Other Poems;* Messrs. William Heinemann Ltd. for *Omega* by GEORGE ROSTREVOR HAMILTON from

Landscape of the Mind; Messrs. Laurence Pollinger Ltd. for *The Junk Man* by CARL SANDBURG from *Chicago Poems* published by Jonathan Cape Ltd., by permission of Holt, Rinehart and Winston Inc., *Only Man* by D. H. LAWRENCE from *The Complete Poems of D. H. Lawrence* published by William Heinemann Ltd. by permission of the Estate of the late Mrs. Frieda Lawrence; The Society of Authors as literary representatives of the Estate of the late A. E. Housman and Messrs. Jonathan Cape Ltd. publishers of A. E. Housman's *Collected Poems* for *When Israel out of Egypt Came* by A. E. HOUSMAN; Messrs. Rupert Hart-Davis Ltd. for an extract from *Nicodemus* by ANDREW YOUNG, *In a Country Church* by R. E. THOMAS from *Songs at the Year's Turning*; Messrs. Sheed and Ward Ltd. for *Circle of a Girl's Arms, The Young Man,* and *God Abides in Men* by CARYLL HOUSLANDER from *The Flowering Tree*; Messrs A. P. Watt and Son for *On Righteous Indignation* from *Collected Poems* of G. K. CHESTERTON published by Methuen and Co. Ltd., *The Indian upon God* from *Collected Poems* of W. B. YEATS by permission of Mr. M. B. Yeats and Messrs. MacMillan and Co. Ltd. *In the Wilderness* by ROBERT GRAVES from *Collected Poems 1965* published by Cassell and Co. Ltd.; by permission of Mr. Robert Graves; Messrs. Constable Ltd., for *The Apple Tree* by OLIVER ST. JOHN GOGARTY; Messrs Geoffrey Bles Ltd. for *The Adam Unparadised* and *The Late Passenger* from *Poems* by C. S. LEWIS; The Hogarth Press Ltd. for *Three Christmas Trees* and *A Hymn for Eve* by TERENCE TILLER from *Reading a Medal*; Messrs. Secker and Warburg Ltd. for an extract from *Resurrection* from *Europa and the Bull* by W. R. RODGERS; Messrs. Routledge and Kegan Paul Ltd. for *St. John Baptist* by SIDNEY KEYES; The Bodley Head for *Good Friday Night* from *The Return and Other Poems* by MARGARET WOODS, *To the Sun* by ROY CAMPBELL from *Collected Poems Vol. 1*; The Cresset Press for *Father to the Man* and *And Because* by JOHN KNIGHT from *Straight Lines and Unicorns*; Pegasus Press Ltd. for *On the Swag* by R. A. K. MASON from *Collected Poems* published by Pegasus Press, New Zealand; Associated Book Publishers Ltd. and Methuen and Co. Ltd. for *Christ in the Clay Pit* by JACK CLEMO; Messrs. Harper Row for *Simon the Cyrenian Speaks* from *On These I Stand* by COUNTEE CULLEN, copyright 1925 by Harper and Brothers, renewed 1953 by Ida M. Cullen, reprinted by permission of Harper and Row, publishers; New Directions Publishing Corp. for *Figures for an Apocalypse* by THOMAS MERTON, copyright 1947 by New Directions, reprinted by permission of New Directions Publishing Corporation, New York; SIEGFRID SASSOON for *The Power and the Glory*; PHYLLIS HARTNOLL for *The Mammon of Unrighteousness* and *Bethlehem*; Mrs. Gwyneth Redwood Anderson for *Before Ararat* by JOHN REDWOOD ANDERSON; SUSAN GLYN for *The Seventh Day;* GEOFFREY DEARMER for *Epstein's Madonna and Child;* JOHN LEO KENNEDY for *Words for a Resurrection;* EDWIN MORGAN for *Good Friday;* THOMAS BLACKBURN for *The Judas Tree;* Mrs. A. Johnson for *Easter Folk Song* by GEOFFREY JOHNSON; M. K. JOSEPH for *The New Moses;* TERESA HOOLEY for *Christ in Woolworths;* T. W. RAMSEY for *Pharaoh's Daughter;* PHOEBE HESKETH for *Imagination, Retro me, Sathanas* and *Cabbages*

Museum of Fine Arts, Boston, U.S.A., for *Where do we come from? Who are we? Where are we going?* by PAUL GAUGUIN; the Pergamon Press, Ltd. for *The Cosmos,* by FRANK J. MALINA; ILSA RODMELL for *Eve; Naoh's Ark* tapestry, by ELISABETH BAILLON, courtesy Contemporary Christian

ACKNOWLEDGEMENTS

Art, Inc., New York, photograph by MARGE KANE; The Nolde Foundation, Seebüll for *Pharaoh's Daughter finds Moses,* by ADA and EMILE NOLDE: SUSAN GLYN for *The Annunciation,* Mrs H. Brook and Arthur Tooth & Sons Ltd., for *Christ in the Wilderness – Foxes,* by STANLEY SPENCER; the Reverend Father J. Ethrington for *The Crucifixion,* by GRAHAM SUTHERLAND, O.M.; A. Reynolds Morse for *Geopoliticus Child watches the birth of the New Man,* by SALVADOR DALI; the Provost and Chapter of Coventry Cathedral and P. W. Thompson, Ltd. for the *Baptistry Window,* by JOHN PIPER; Reinhold Publishing Corporation, New York, for photograph of *The Church of Our Lady of Grace, Assy.*

INDEX OF FIRST LINES